D0241833

Ite
s
b
tele
barc
This
Rene
Fine
incurre
be cha

Le

DIFFERENT CLASS

My Favourite Sporting Heroes

Brainse Fhionnglaise   Finglas Library
T: (01) 834 4906 E: finglaslibrary@dublincity.ie

DIFFERENT CLASS

My Favourite Sporting Heroes

JIMMY MAGEE
WITH JASON O'TOOLE ~

Withdrawn From Stock
Dublin Public Libraries

Gill & Macmillan

Gill & Macmillan
Hume Avenue, Park West, Dublin 12
with associated companies throughout the world
www.gillmacmillanbooks.ie

© Jimmy Magee 2013
978 07171 5858 4

Index compiled by Fionbar Lyons
Typography design by Make Communication
Print origination by Carole Lynch
Printed and bound by CPI Group (UK) Ltd, CR0 4YY

This book is typeset in Linotype Minion and
Neue Helvetica.

The paper used in this book comes from the wood
pulp of managed forests. For every tree felled, at
least one tree is planted, thereby renewing natural
resources.

All rights reserved. No part of this publication may
be copied, reproduced or transmitted in any form
or by any means, without permission of the
publishers.

A CIP catalogue record for this book is available
from the British Library.

5 4 3 2 1

CONTENTS

ACKNOWLEDGEMENTS

I would like to thank Ciara for transcribing the tapes and also the management and staff of the Stephen's Green Hibernian Club, where I had the pleasure of working on this book.

Chapter 1 ∿

| MY FAVOURITE SPORTS STARS

I said it almost thirty years ago, but people still quote back to me my famous description of Maradona being a *different class* during the infamous 'Hand of God' game. The *different class* reference is one that I'm constantly reminded of, because every time I walk into the RTE studio I immediately see it displayed in giant letters on the wall in reception.

Who'll ever forget watching Maradona take the ball in his own half and dribble past five English players, including the goalkeeper, Peter Shilton, to score one of the most spectacular goals ever? It was rightly voted Goal of the Century during an on-line poll by FIFA.com in 2002.

My on-air comment is something that sports fans always remind me about; and then usually they ask me who else in sport, by my estimation, is a *different class,* and, more importantly, what makes them so.

It's not a straightforward question to answer. In my opinion, to be worthy of such a great accolade a sports star first and foremost has to be supreme in their own chosen field and be consistently winning major medals in all championships—be it national or continental, or more specifically at the global level, the likes of the World Cup and the Olympics. And not only must they reach such a summit but they must possess a special or unique talent in what they do, as with the aforementioned Maradona goal.

These figures almost always transcend their own sport and are universally revered as cultural icons, like rock stars or Hollywood royalty, and are immediately recognisable by virtually everyone on the planet, not just sports fans. You could drop the likes of Muhammad Ali or Pelé into a remote village in Africa with no television and I'd bet you that they would still be recognised.

Leabharlanna Poibli Chathair Bhaile Átha Cliath
Dublin City Public Libraries

With no further ado, I present to you over the next two chapters my list of those who I consider to be the top fifteen sports stars in living memory.

1. MUHAMMAD ALI

He ticks all the right boxes. Muhammad Ali had footwork that would do credit to a professional tap dancer and the hand speed of a flyweight. He could feint and shuffle at amazing angles and speed for such a big man. (He was 6 feet 2 inches and at his peak about 15 stone.)

He had a confidence that verged on arrogance, but nobody can deny that here was a boxer able to back up his bragging with a ringful of victories. His professional career spanned twenty years, from 1961 to 1981, with a career tally of 61 fights, with 56 wins (of which 37 were KOs) and 5 losses. He won the world championship three times.

He was famously stripped of his world belt in 1967 for refusing to join the US army to fight in Vietnam, his comment at the time being, 'Man, I ain't got no quarrel with them Viet Cong. I'm not going ten thousand miles from home to help murder and burn another poor nation simply to continue the domination of white slavemasters of the darker people the world over.' I admired him at the time for that, because he stood up for what he believed, despite the fact that it had a negative effect on his early career.

He met all the big names in boxing, but perhaps the greatest of all fights was his comeback against Smokin' Joe Frazier at Madison Square Garden in 1971. He lost that one, but he came back stronger to beat Frazier in a rematch in 1974 and reclaim his title as undisputed world champion. Muhammad Ali was the greatest

I first met Ali when he came to Dublin to fight at Croke Park in 1972 and interviewed him several times over the subsequent years. My fondest memory of him is when I saw him perform the opening ceremony at the 1996 Olympics in Atlanta. It was really emotional to see him back on the Olympic stage after he had thrown his Olympic medal in disgust into the Ohio River because he couldn't get served at a 'whites-only' restaurant in his native city. I couldn't blame him. (The

International Olympic Committee did give him a new medal to replace it, but I don't know if he threw that one away also.) So, all those years later, it must have been a poignant moment for him to receive such respect and applause back in his native South at the Olympic Games, which is without doubt the biggest event ever to take place in the Southern States.

The greatest fight that never took place is probably the one between Cassius Clay (as he was called then) and Teófilo Stevenson of Cuba, who won the Olympic heavyweight division three times in a row in 1972, 1976 and 1980. That was some achievement! There was a big push for him to fight Clay. They were the two best heavyweights in the world at the time, even though one was an amateur and the other a pro, and people really wanted to see how these two most talked-about pugilists would fight each other.

For many reasons, none of which I know for certain, Stevenson's people would not allow him to box. Perhaps they had cold feet— and who could blame them? Cassius probably would have won, but Stevenson was a wonderful boxer, who only died in 2012. I wanted to go to Cuba to meet him at one time but, sadly, never got the opportunity.

Muhammad Ali was brilliant on his feet but maybe not so great against powerhouse boxers. Stevenson was a powerhouse-style of boxer, but he was equally excellent on his feet. In fact he was so good in the Munich 1972 Olympics that the fella he was supposed to fight in the final withdrew, because of a supposed injured hand. I have my doubts about that alleged injury and reckon he ran scared because Stevenson was just putting fellas away for fun at that stage in his career.

There was an American guy named Duane Bobick, who was one of the new white hopes (and white he was too, which was unusual for an American heavyweight champion). The Americans thought he was going to be the bee's knees, and the famous American broadcaster Howard Cosell, since deceased, was boasting about him all during the Olympics and all over the Olympic Village in Munich. Bobick met Stevenson in the quarter-final, and he was hammered; Stevenson took him apart and eventually put him away. It cost Bobick a million dollars, because he had signed a pre-games contract. A million dollars in 1972 was huge money. The presumptuous deal was that he would turn pro when he won the Olympics, and there was no 'if' in it when he met the Cuban, who put an end to that dream.

Ali is such a famous face and personality . . . as I say, I guess you could drop him out of a plane in the world's most remote land, and the first person to approach him would immediately know he was Muhammad Ali. That's what I call a *different class*.

2. EDDY MERCKX

He is undoubtedly the greatest racing cyclist of all time and Belgium's most adored sportsman. Belgium is a country that is culturally split, but both the Dutch-speaking Flemings and the French-speaking Walloons have attached themselves and endeared themselves to Eddy Merckx, who was born in Brussels but is of Flemish parentage. When asked—and he has been asked on numerous occasions—'Which are you? Are you Flemish or Wallonian?' he always diplomatically gives the same response: 'I am a Belgian.'

He was a sex symbol too in his home country and looked a ringer for Elvis Presley, thanks to the shape of his face and his dark hair and curls.

He won the Tour de France an impressive five times and also on five occasions triumphed in the Giro d'Italia, as well as winning three world championships. He won ninety-one yellow jerseys, three green jerseys and dozens of stage victories, which is an unbelievable record. He has held the hour record too.

Merckx made history in the 1969 Tour de France by collecting the yellow, green and red polka-dot jerseys. The yellow jersey is the daily one worn by the race leader, the polka-dot one is held by the best climber and the green one is the points jersey for the most consistent finisher. Amazingly, not only did he hold all three during that race but he won all three outright, which is an astonishing feat that no-one else has ever achieved. He was so good that the triumph of the triple jersey is unique and unbeaten and unlikely ever to be: not even Lance Armstrong on drugs could match him!

What made him all the more remarkable is that he usually didn't really depend on team work or tactics: he was so good and so strong that he would just dash off and leave the others eating his dust. He wasn't in sight of anyone at all one time when he won a stage by a staggering twenty minutes. His power and pace were unmatchable. He was just superior.

In his heyday he did everything. But despite all the success the French didn't warm to him, because they didn't like to see their Tour de France being won by a Belgian. They began to cheer him only after one terrible incident near the end of his career, which summed up his steely determination. An idiot ran out onto the road and punched him in the belly on a Tour stage. It flattened him. Badly hurt, he got up, dusted himself off, and insisted on finishing the stage. Even with a burst gut after being assaulted, Mercky somehow found the inner strength to get to the finishing line—not only that, but he still came second, which is a real measure of the man. From that moment on he got massive support in France.

During my first Tour de France I met Merckx when I was introduced to him by a Belgian journalist friend of mine. In fact on that first morning of the Tour de France Merckx left me holding his bike as he went off to register. I still pinch myself when I think about it now. Years after our first meeting Merckx invited me to his home, where he made his famous bikes. It was amazing being inside the house, half of which was a bike factory and the other half his living quarters. He was truly a *different class.*

3. JACK NICKLAUS

Jack Nicklaus, dubbed the Golden Bear, was only twenty-two when he won his first of four US Opens in 1962, and then the following year he won the first of his six Masters and also the US Open again. He was forty-six when he won his eighteenth major victory in 1986. It's a record that still hasn't been matched, with Tiger Woods being the only golfer who could conceivably catch up with it at the moment.

What's equally impressive is Jack's runner-up statistics. He has been runner-up in majors more times than anyone else. So, if you take his overall record for first and second there is hardly room for anyone else.

On a number of occasions he has been generous with his time when I have sought interviews with him at the major tournaments, such as Merion in 1981, at the US Open, at the 1983 Ryder Cup at Muirfield, and the 1984 Masters at Augusta National. But I actually had to turn down the first time we were supposed to meet for an interview, back in 1970 at the British Open (correctly, the Open Championship) in St Andrews, because it clashed with a report I had to do for RTE News. Nicklaus told me, 'We will do it again.' And, true to his word, three years later, at the 1973 Ryder Cup in Muirfield, he immediately said when he saw me, 'Would you like to do that interview now?' I couldn't believe that the number 1 golfer in the world could remember meeting me briefly three years previously.

After the interview I was strolling around the course with some journalists and we spotted Nicklaus on the fairway with Lee Trevino, Billy Casper, and Arnold Palmer. It was one of those Hall of Fame type moments. The Golden Bear spotted me and shouted out, 'Hello, Jimmy!' I said hello back, and everybody turned to me and asked, 'How do you know Jack Nicklaus?' Neglecting to tell them that I had only interviewed him ten minutes earlier, I replied with a little white lie: 'Ah, sure we've been mates a long time!'

Nicklaus is far ahead of everybody else, apart from Tiger Woods, who is still four majors behind him. Even if Tiger did overtake him I would still probably regard Nicklaus as my all-time favourite golfer.

4. PELÉ

The first footballer on my list is the great Brazilian Edison Arantes do Nascimento, better known by his sobriquet Pelé. In 1999 he was voted Player of the Century by the International Federation of Football History and Statistics, and he consistently tops virtually every opinion poll.

He was first capped for Brazil when he was sixteen and won the World Cup for the first time at seventeen. He was really only a child in that final but he still managed to show his *different class* by scoring twice. And he then cried like a child when they won it in 1958, and one of the older players had to console him. He is the only player in the history of the beautiful game to win three World Cups, after FIFA retrospectively awarded him a medal for the 1962 World Cup, in which he was injured during the second group game in the competition. It's a feat that will probably never be equalled.

I first met him face to face in 1974 in Frankfurt, when we had a great chat, and then we met again in a television studio in São Paulo in 1977. My friend Walter Abreu, who had me in to do an interview for his television show, told me when I arrived, 'I have someone to meet you.' He then brought me up to meet the living legend, who is one of only two of my heroes that I ever bothered asking for an autograph—the other being Maradona. That's how much reverence I hold for him. Another time I visited Brazil my friend Walter had Pelé record a video greeting to welcome me to Brazil. I have met him many times since, and he now knows me, which I think is good. I have to pinch myself when I think how I'm on first-name terms with such an iconic figure.

The old adage about how you should never meet your heroes is far from true in the case of Pelé, a humble man despite his global fame. The following story sums up for me how modest he is. When the Brazilian team visited Dublin back in the 1970s I decided to go out to Terenure, where they were training at the college, to say hello to Pelé. I discovered him on his own in the church, deep in prayer. I waited for him to come out, and he told me that he always prayed whenever he can to thank God. 'I am a lucky man,' he told me.

I like to joke about how I came up with Pelé's nickname. I remember asking him once how he got his nickname. I asked him, 'Was it a flower? A small animal?'

He replied: 'There is no meaning to it. It means nothing. And as a child I hated the name and used to get into fights in school when other boys called me "Pelé", because I thought it was derogatory. At home they called me another name.'

I told him I had an idea of how he might have got the moniker. Amused, he listened intently as I rumbled on with a story. 'There was a missionary Catholic priest, and he was on a mission in Brazil near

Santos, where Pelé was raised. Your family were very poor, and you were playing with a cloth or paper ball and you were fantastic with it, and the priest saw you. He was an Irish-speaking priest, and he said, "Look at the buachaill ag imirt peile," which means playing football. And all the oul ones were around and going, "Ahh! Pelé! Pelé! Pelé!" And when the priest was gone the name stuck. Now isn't that a plausible story?'

He laughed and agreed it was as likely as any of the other stories he heard. When I met him again, this time in Brussels to make a present-ation to Johan Cruyff, Pelé jokingly asked me, 'How's my Irish priest's friend?'

I smiled when I discovered how he included a section on my Irish priest in his autobiography! Many people seem to believe it's a true story; it's all over the internet now as fact. Of course it's not, but it shows you how a story can grow legs.

5. CARL LEWIS

When I was a child my father told me about the great Jesse Owens. 'There will never be another one like him.' It was hard to imagine any-one replicating Owens's spectacular achievement of four gold medals at the 1936 Olympic Games in Berlin. It took almost fifty years to happen again, when Carl Lewis took four golds at the 1984 Olympics in Los Angeles. He also has the distinction of being joint second for number of Olympic medals, with his nine gold and one bronze.

I immediately knew Lewis was special when I did the commentary at the 1983 World Track and Field Championships in Helsinki. He was the rising new star, anchoring the American 4 × 100 relay team and winning the two sprints and the long jump. It's the long jump that he has left as his challenge for future decades. We exchanged a few words at the press conference. He had the world at his feet, and he knew it. I asked him what he really wanted to do, and he told me he wanted to replicate Jesse Owens's 1936 Olympic medal haul, when Owens won four gold medals. He said that if he looked after himself he felt he might be able to do it. However, people thought it was an outlandish claim for some upstart to think he would be as good as Jesse Owens: but he has proved that he is every bit as good as that.

I was in Los Angeles in 1984 when he equalled Jesse Owens's record by winning the 100, 200, long jump and 4 × 100 relay. The big thing he wanted to do, apart from the Jesse Owens record, was to reach 30 feet in the long jump, which had never been attained—and still hasn't. He suggested that it was possible, and he also says that he did it once in Indianapolis. I investigated this and discovered that he did in fact reach 30 feet, but they had to cross the tape and the board, and there was a mark on the plasticine, and this made them deem it a foul. But all the same he was right about reaching the 30-foot mark. It has still never been officially achieved in competition.

The long jump is a major part of him: he won it in 1984, 1988, 1992 and 1996—a staggering four times in a row, the last one when he was thirty-six years old. So for me, that and his style make Carl Lewis the greatest athlete of them all for variety and longevity, and his medal collection: nine Olympic gold medals and eight world titles. Nobody can hold a candle to that.

Trivia buffs will probably get a kick out of this little nugget. Carl has a sister who is also an athlete. Her name—wait for it—is Carol!

6. TIGER WOODS

Tiger Woods, in my opinion, is probably the only golfer at the moment who can realistically catch up with Jack Nicklaus's remarkable record.

So commanding was Tiger at the fabled Augusta National in the second full week of April 1997 (it's always held in the second week of April) that he won it with the amazing stats of 12 under par on 270 for 72 holes. It was a magnificent record-breaking performance.

I can still vividly remember the morning of his first round of that famous victory that announced his arrival as a serious contender in the golfing world. I had got up at the crack of dawn, because I wanted to catch as much golf as possible. For some reason I had got it into my head—and don't forget, this chap was only coming up on twenty-one years of age—that Tiger was going to win the Masters. Most people who

I mentioned this to seemed to think I was going insane to be building up Tiger, who had only turned professional the year previously, and they didn't bother getting up early to watch his first round. It was their loss.

But I had to see him, because my gut instinct was telling me that Tiger was special. I got a lift to the course with the hotel transport and I caught up with Tiger on the first fairway to see this marvellous young fella tee off for that historic first Masters victory.

'God, it's only starting but it's all over for him already!' I remember thinking when he took forty shots to the turn, and he ended up being four over par at the end of the first. So I said to myself, that was the end of that dream. But I wasn't going to desert him now that he was down, and I stuck it out to see if he could claw his way back into the game. He came back in 30 shots for 70. Soon all my colleagues, who had originally dismissed my prediction, were talking Tiger up too.

And three days later he was the Masters champion, at the tender age of twenty-one, which makes him the youngest golfer to win the top competition at Augusta. He was so good that they had to do a job fixing up the famous course afterwards, because he took it to pieces and made it look like a pitch-and-putt course!

At the press conference afterwards I said to him, 'Tiger, judging by the margin of your victory and the way you hit the ball, could you have won the Masters with just four clubs in your bag?'

He looked at me and smiled. 'How many holes would I have to play?' he asked me.

'That's a diplomatic answer,' I replied.

'I'm trying to be diplomatic!'

Make what you will of that!

7. USAIN BOLT

Widely regarded as the fastest man on the planet, Usain Bolt has electri-fied sprinting since his sensational clock-bashing runs in the Bird's Nest stadium in Beijing in 2008. His world record times at that Olympics were 9.69 for the 100 metres and 19.30 for the 200 metres. He is the only runner to hold world records in both the 100 and the 200 metres since the fully automatic time measurement became mandatory back in the late 1970s.

The great Tommie Smith—who memorably won gold at the 1968 Olympics in Mexico, which will always be remembered for the image of him with his so-called Black Power salute protest at the medal ceremony—said before that run: 'Bolt will surprise everyone, because he will beat Michael Johnson's time.'

Now, everybody was a little taken aback by this prediction, because Michael Johnson had done it in 19.32 in Atlanta. But Tommie Smith was adamant when he met me before the race in Beijing that Bolt would do it.

He won the 100 metres, yet surprisingly he was probably the slowest to react coming out of the block; but he was still half a metre ahead of all the other runners at 40 metres. He then slowed up with about 20 metres to go, lowered his arms, and began celebrating, so there is no knowing now what time he could have done it in. As it is, he let the clock run down in that run. I asked him afterwards, 'Is this the limit that a man can do?'

'No. I will be back in four years, and I will win them again—hopefully,' he replied, crossing his fingers.

True enough, the Jamaican runner nicknamed 'Lightning Bolt' was back in London in 2012 and won them again. He has six gold medals from the previous two Olympics and five gold medals from the world championship. You can safely put your money on him winning more gold medals at the next Olympics in Rio. This man is certainly a *different class*.

Brainse Fhionnglaise   Finglas Library
T: (01) 834 4906 E: finglaslibrary@dublincity.ie

Chapter 2 ~

| MORE SENSATIONAL TALENTS

I'm at the half-way stage of listing my all-time favourite sports stars, but any one of the next eight could probably justify, or make, a strong case to be in a higher position in my top fifteen, and none more so than the little Argentine next on my list, who inspired the title of the book you are holding in your hands.

A good friend of mine said to me that I should have Maradona at number 1 in my list of the greatest players ever. But I replied, 'Ah, not really.'

He then retorted, 'Sure you wouldn't be calling this book *Different Class* if it wasn't for Maradona! Isn't that where you got the title from?'

It's a fair point. Yes, Maradona was a *different class*, as I memorably pointed out when doing the commentary for the infamous 'Hand of God' match—which I'm now going to rename the famous 'Feet of God' game—against England; but not everybody can be number 1 in my list of footballers. That honour falls to Pelé.

8. DIEGO MARADONA

Season after storied season, football gives us one or two or, if we're very lucky, three new sensational talents. In no particular order, the best players for my money are Matthews, Stefano, Puskás, Greaves, Gento, Pelé, Eusébio, Bobby Charlton, Law, Cruyff, Platini, van Basten, Ronaldo, the younger Messi and, last but not least, Diego Maradona.

So who is the best? It's a common question, to which there is no answer that can be conclusive; however, I still haven't seen any better than Argentina's golden boy, Diego Maradona. Yes, I know, I have Pelé at number 4 on this list, but you could possibly argue that it's a biased opinion and that Maradona is equally good. I believe Pelé edges it, but

I'm open to persuasion on this. After all, Maradona scored what is probably the greatest goal in the history of the game, against England in Mexico in '86.

Perhaps Maradona might have surpassed Pelé on this list if he had achieved more, rather than being mired in so much controversy in the later stage of his career, such as being expelled from the 1994 World Cup after he tested positive for a so-called 'cocktail of drugs', which included ephedrine, a weight-loss drug.

I honestly think it was an absolute disgrace on the part of FIFA to do this. As I said in my previous book, *Memory Man*, Maradona was made a scapegoat by FIFA with his undeserved expulsion from that World Cup. It was actually a news report that I did in which the term 'cocktail of drugs' first surfaced, after I had done an interview with the person in charge of the decision to send Maradona packing. I was the one who quoted the phrase that all the papers went with.

The reason I am adamant that Maradona was made a scapegoat is that immediately after he was booted out I spoke to a pharmacist, who told me that with this particular drug you would want to 'take the entire shop's stock' to lose any significant weight in an effort to enhance your performance on the pitch. We could hardly accuse Maradona of being anorexic at that stage in his career!

I am not daring to suggest for one moment that Maradona didn't take this stupid stuff, and I am certainly not suggesting it wasn't illegal, but I felt if he was at it, then others were probably at it also. But they needed to get a big scalp, and Maradona was the biggest scalp you could get—just as Ben Johnson was in the 1988 Olympic Games. I do believe Johnson took stuff, but then when he was stripped of his gold medal and subsequently everybody else behind him was moved up one slot, if you look at their later CVs, those athletes were not lily-white at all either.

The big question is, Would Argentina have won that tournament with him? Probably not; but still it was a shame to see such a talented player booted out unceremoniously and never afforded the opportunity to play at that high level again. Personally, I was disappointed not to have Maradona there on the world stage. At the very least he would have brought some excitement and much-needed skill to the tournament. Let's be honest: it certainly wasn't the most memorable World Cup for pure skill.

I first realised how special Maradona was when I visited Buenos Aires back in 1977 and decided to go to a local football match between Argentina Juniors and Velez Sarsfields and came across a certain up-and-coming sixteen-year old named Diego Maradona on the team sheet. I will always remember how, after half time, a chubby sub with bushy hair ran onto the pitch. But he was just sensational. At first I didn't pay any attention to him, but soon he had tickled my interest with his sublime skill, and I started telling myself, 'This fella is unbelievable; he can do anything.'

I knew even then that this kid was going to be an international sensation. They don't have programmes at matches in South America as they have here. I think that is based on the principle that all the home supporters know their own team, and they don't give a damn about the others. It has to be that. But there's a magazine there called *El Gráfico*, which is essentially a football magazine with some other sports thrown in. It had these marks out of ten, which is now popular everywhere around the world; but they were very conservative, to such an extent that even if you played really well you would get a maximum of seven out of ten at most, averaging about six. Everybody seemed to get a five or six, unless they were exceptional.

That night, after seeing Maradona in the flesh, I waited in Avenida Florida for when the latest editions of the magazines and newspapers would hit the news-stands at about midnight. I grabbed a copy of *El Gráfico*, which came out every week and after special matches. The ink was still damp, and I looked up the match I had seen earlier. There was the name: Diego Armando Maradona. He played only half the match, and he was awarded nine in the ratings in this magazine. I thought to myself, 'This backs everything I thought when I saw him play.'

I'm open to correction, but I probably did the first piece ever on Maradona for a European publication when I wrote about him for my next column in the *Sunday World*. I said something along the lines of 'Watch out for this fella in the World Cup, 1978. He is going to be the sensation of the tournament.' Sure enough, a year later Maradona was in the Argentine squad. They thought he was too young to play in the World Cup, so sadly he didn't get any match time. Those who had heard me off-air talking about him said, 'Ah, sure that was a lucky guess! Did you really see him play at all?'

I told them: 'Mark my words. You may have to wait another four years, but he will be there. He is the next great player.'

I was eventually proved right when he arrived on the international scene in 1982 and single-handedly beat England in 1986 with his *different class*, as I described it when doing the commentary on that game. Again in 1986 he was a one-man orchestra and soloist as captain when Argentina won the World Cup.

As history shows, even his God-given talents couldn't protect him from drugs, largely to do with weight control; but clean or dirty, the little man could make the ball talk, and that ball had a one-word vocabulary: Maradona.

For me, Pelé and Maradona would be the two biggest players ever to grace the game.

9. SUGAR RAY ROBINSON

Without doubt, Sugar Ray Robinson can justifiably be described as one of the greatest boxers of all time. For my money he is second, behind Muhammad Ali. He was named Boxer of the Decade in the 1980s.

Sugar was born Walker Smith and trained at a gym in Harlem, New York. When he was only fifteen he was already waiting for a chance to box professionally, and less than a year later he had his first contest, but he was under age: you're not allowed to box under the age of sixteen. To get the fight Walker had to get the identity card of another boxer, who, luckily for him, didn't turn up to the weigh-in. The other boxer was called Ray Robinson. The name stuck.

Robinson got into the ring, and one old-time reporter (there's always an old-time reporter in America) was very impressed with this child boxer and said, 'He's as sweet as sugar.' And that name stuck also; so from then on he was called Sugar Ray Robinson. He went in as Walker Smith and came out as Sugar Ray Robinson.

What followed was a 25-year career of 201 professional fights, including 21 world title bouts. In most lists of the world's greatest fighters Robinson is up there in everyone's top three, and most often their number 1 or 2. He had the best left hand in the fight game. He was welterweight champion, 1946–50, and middleweight champion until 1961. He had the dancing feet of Bo Jangles, the nerves of a fighter pilot, and the looks of a film star.

I had the pleasure of meeting Sugar Ray when his career was finished. I was in New York with some boxing people; we were in Jack Dempsey's place (former heavyweight champion of the world) on Broadway. Sugar still looked like a film star when I saw him and was able to shake hands with him. (I wasn't going to wash my hands for ages after shaking his hand. I shook his right hand, and he was famous for his left hand, so I thought, 'What the hell. I'll wash it!') He didn't really say a whole lot, just 'Terrific to meet you,' etc. He struck me as being very mannerly, like most Americans. There was no big ego with this gentle giant.

Robinson was a heroic figure: he was amazing, really. He was and still is the greatest pound-for-pound boxer of all time.

10. EDWIN MOSES

Edwin Moses is the 'winningest' (a very American word that I have never used before now) one-lap hurdler that athletics has ever seen. This American athlete was the greatest 400-metres hurdler in the sport's history, holding on to his world record for donkeys' years.

His style was rare, if not unique: a thirteen-stride pattern between hurdles. And his cv is all but unbelievable: in nine years, nine months and nine days he didn't lose a race at all at 400-metres hurdles. An extraordinary achievement!

He won the Olympic Games in Montreal in 1976. Sadly, he never got to participate in the 1980 Moscow Olympics, because the United

States decided to boycott it over the Soviet Union's intervention in Afghanistan. (The irony of this can't surely be lost on anybody in the light of the Americans then invading Afghanistan.)

Moses was back in form in Los Angeles in 1984, where he won gold again. Apart from his two gold medals and one bronze at these two Olympics he also came first during the world championships in Helsinki in 1983 and in Rome in 1987.

I became a close acquaintance of his during the shooting of the international television show 'The Superstars', which he competed in and for which I was the presenter for RTE. You could tell that he was taking part in all the events for fun. He was very helpful to me in the making of the programme, bending over backwards to assist me with the filming, which was a real measure of the man.

I will always remember this funny story about him. During the Olympics in Los Angeles in 1984 I was outside the gates of the Coliseum one day waiting for the traffic lights to change so as to cross the street, and right up beside me was Ed Moses.

As we stood at the traffic lights a car pulled up in front of us in which there were three or four Irishmen, who called out to me. I noticed that in the car was Bob Tisdall, who, fifty-two years before, won gold at the 400-metres hurdles in the same event and on the same track as the man beside me, Ed Moses!

There wouldn't have been more than three yards between the car and where Ed Moses was standing; in that space were the only two men who had won the 400 metres in the same stadium. The Olympic Games were held on the same track, in the Coliseum in Los Angeles, in 1932 and 1984, which is the only time that ever happened, before or since.

It was one of those moments when you wish you had a camera— one of those pinch-yourself moments. In retrospect, I wish I had had the good sense to say to Ed Moses, 'Here's a special man I want you to meet,' and stop the car. But it was just too awkward, because the lights changed quickly and the car had to move on. Neither of them knew the other was there, and yet there were only a few yards between them and this historic moment for a sports buff like me.

Today Ed Moses is a very strong anti-drugs campaigner. He is attached to the International Olympic Committee and he works as kind of a drug detective. Wherever he gets the chance to speak out he will do so.

That's Edwin Moses—a *different class.*

11. MICHAEL JORDAN

The National Basketball Association itself proclaims Michael Jordan 'the greatest basketball player of all time.' While still a student, he won his first gold medal at the 1984 Olympics and then went on to play for the 'Dream Team' that won gold at Barcelona in 1992. That team oozed talent, such as Magic Johnson, Karl Malone (nicknamed the Mailman) and Larry Bird. It was a team of All-Stars, but Jordan was the brightest jewel in the cache, and was the only one to start all eight games at the '92 Olympics.

In each element Jordan, an NBA winner on six occasions, was the best at dunking, passing, low passes—virtually everything that could be done on the court.

I met him briefly in New York at an All-Stars game and he reminded me of the occasion in 1992 in Barcelona when the United States were playing their first game against Angola. Laughing at the recollection, Jordan recounted how they were warming up on court, and all the Angolan players had cameras and they were all taking pictures of Jordan and Team USA. 'I couldn't believe it that some of the Angolan team were asking me for my autograph before the game!' Jordan told me.

The American team signed the autographs, and I'm sure the Angolans say, 'You would want to have been with us the day we met so-and-so.'

Jordan is the only player I've ever seen on the court receive a standing ovation from opposition fans. Now that is, in my book, a *different class* of player.

12. MICHAEL SCHUMACHER

I've been blessed to see so many spectacular drivers on the Formula One tracks. The names that immediately jump to mind are Alain Prost,

Fernando Alonso, Juan Manuel Fangio, Nelson Piquet, Damon Hill, Lewis Hamilton, Ayrton Senna and Nigel Mansell. But the one that jumps to mind the most out of all these is Michael Schumacher.

The German prodigy's record speaks for itself. He has won more than three hundred Formula One races, with 91 grand prix wins—making him the driver with the greatest number of grand prix victories in the sport's history—and 68 pole positions. With seven world championships under his belt, it's really hard to think of anybody who can hold a candle to this fantastic driver. Even the man second in the all-time list, Alain Prost, has only 51 grand prix victories, compared with Schumacher's 91, with the third-placed Ayrton Senna chalking up only 41 wins, less than half the German's total. That in itself speaks volumes about his record.

It's nice to know that there is an Irish connection here. The first Formula One race Schumacher had was for the Irish maverick Eddie Jordan in 1991 at Spa-Francorchamps.

Like a lot of people who don't like talking about their own sport when they are off the track or field, Schumacher loved talking about football. I talked football with him one time in Catalonia, at the Barcelona grand prix. He knew a lot about it. I got the impression from our chat that he really wanted to be a footballer, but he said he wasn't good enough. He might not have been good enough to play along with the fellas that he was talking about, such as Gerd Müller, Franz Beckenbauer, etc., but I'd imagine he probably wasn't half bad as a youngster. Still, football's loss was certainly Formula One's gain.

13. SEVE BALLESTEROS

Sadly, Seve Ballesteros died at the age of fifty-four back in 2011. He was one of the most charismatic golfers I ever had the pleasure of observing up close and personal—no doubt about that.

When he played in the Irish Open at Portmarnock I was determined to get an interview with him, but he had yet to learn English at that time, which was his very early days in the game, and spoke only his native Spanish. I got an interpreter whom I knew, and we got a room and sat down and talked away. He was very forthcoming, but it was a slow process. I asked him if he knew how much money he had made in the last year. I would say, 'Oh, you won £17,500?'

'No,' he immediately replied in perfect English, 'I won £19,000!' So, the only parts of English that he spoke very well alluded to finance!

But he was a very nice man and very helpful. Like a lot of people you meet in these situations, we met again, and when we would bump into each other again he recognised me and said thank you for the interview, which tells me in many ways the sort of gentleman he was.

Of course he won a lot more than a mere £19,000, as he went on to become the world's number 1 and won two Masters and three Opens in Britain.

14. JOHAN CRUYFF

I have the Netherlands' greatest footballer at number 14 in this list, for a good reason: because that is the number he wore when he was playing!

He led the Netherlands Total Football team in the final of the 1974 World Cup, a competition in which he excelled. Known for his move dubbed the 'Cruyff turn', when he would drag the ball behind his foot and do a 180-degree turn, he could turn on a guilder. (I like that!) He could read play like few of his contemporaries; he could read goals, and he scored more than his share.

It was a crying shame that this magnificent Dutch side were unable to win the World Cup. They were a great team, who were in two finals. You just don't know why they didn't win anything: they just weren't good enough on the day, and they met Germany on one occasion and Germany was very good. On the next occasion they met Argentina in Argentina. Unfortunately, Cruyff didn't play in the second one, and he should have, but apparently there was some kidnapping threat made to his family and he decided against travelling to Argentina.

I suppose another reason why the Dutch never seem to live up to the great expectation—apart from Euro '88—is because they were always having rows among themselves, and with anyone else. There was a row during Cruyff's time because they were sponsored by Adidas and there was the War of the Stripes (my own title). Cruyff wouldn't wear Adidas, because he was on a personal contract with Puma and he insisted on wearing Puma boots. If you saw a photo of the Dutch team from that time you would see how they covered up the other thing by turning around his jersey, but the boots are there with two stripes and everyone else had the famous three stripes of Adidas.

He was very much his own man, and a reason like that would also have put him out of Argentina.

As a coach he married his gifts to the talents of Barcelona Football Club. He won eleven trophies while there, including the League four times and the European Cup. It's a record that was only surpassed by one of his former students, Pep Guardiola.

The glorious football emanating from Camp Nou today had its seeds in the inventive brain of the Dutch master Johan Cruyff.

On a personal level I've always liked Cruyff, because he has done a few things for me, like presenting an award for me on one occasion to Pelé. On another occasion he got me into the Ajax dressing-room when he was playing for them. They had won the European Cup and they were playing in the old De Meer field, which was their home ground. I went and asked if I could see Cruyff, and then I asked him if I could see inside. Now, there was nothing to see—it was just another dressing-room—but he was kind enough to bring me in and give me a tour.

The thing that I remembered most about him that surprised me was that he smoked. It was the day of a match and he was smoking away. Later on in life he had a heart problem. I think he had a bypass and he had to give up smoking.

Just to show what a *different class* Cruyff was as a player, he was voted European Player of the Century, and came only second to Pelé in a vote for the greatest player of all time.

15. MICHAEL PHELPS

To be witness as a commentator when Mark Spitz won his seven Olympic gold medals in swimming—each in a record time—is an abiding memory for me of the Munich 1972 Olympics. Most punters reckoned we wouldn't see Spitz's record matched in our lifetime, but then before we knew it along came the 'Albatross' Michael Gross and the 'Torpedo' Ian Thorpe to clean out the pool.

Then almost again before we could take a deep breath—the 'Baltimore Bullet' Michael Phelps, who at nineteen scooped a staggering six-medal jackpot in Athens in 2004. He then returned to surpass this with eight gold medals in Beijing in 2008. Remarkably, he was back for his third Olympics in London in 2012, where he won four gold medals. This brought his winning streak to an unmatchable eighteen gold medals and two silvers (both won in London) and two bronze (at the Athens games). This gives him a grand total of twenty-two Olympic medals—with more gold medals than Ireland has ever won combined. In fact, he has won double the amount of gold medals than the other couple of athletes who are joint second on the all-time list of multiple Olympic gold medallists.

With his 6 foot 7 inches arm span, a height of 6 feet 4 inches and size 14 feet, the parts were disproportionate, to say the least; even these sports specialists can't understand how he could put it all together into one package. He, like all the other stars on this list, is of a *different class*.

Chapter 3 ～

THE UNITED NATIONS OF SPORT

To see the United Nations one can visit New York at any time; but the opportunity to see the united nations of sport—with an estimated two hundred countries participating in the Summer and Winter Games—presents itself only every four years, at different exotic places.

For me it has been a thrilling journey as someone who has been to eleven Summer Olympics and three Winter Olympics, taking in the likes of Athens, Barcelona, Los Angeles, Atlanta, London, Munich, Mexico, Seoul, Montreal, Moscow, Sydney, and Beijing. It is amazing when you are at them: you see so many people around, and then you realise that about 70 per cent of the world's population are following the Olympic Games, either through live television, radio or on line, with the audience for London being something like five billion.

There were 14,700 athletes in London, 4,200 of them Paralympians. When you are at the Olympic Games you are aware of its magnificent history and you think of all the fantastic things that have happened and you really feel you are part of it all.

An apt name for an athlete would be Lane, wouldn't it? Because you run in lanes! Francis Lane was the first winner at the Olympic Games, winning a heat of the 100 metres in Athens in 1896. He wasn't a medallist, though, in the final.

As the world's foremost sports competition, there's as many as twenty-six sports to choose from; of course you can't see them all, but with a bit of military-type planning you can certainly squeeze many different disciplines into one day.

Commenting on the Olympics you are assigned sports to cover, and mine was boxing; but there isn't boxing non-stop, so in the hour or two in between sessions I would go and see other things. I left the ExCel Arena in London in 2012 and went with haste to the Olympic Stadium to catch a potentially historic moment that I wanted to see, but with no guarantee it was going to happen. As it turned out I saw Usain Bolt winning the 200 metres, to complete therefore the sprint double for a unique second time, having won the 100 and 200 in Beijing four years previously.

In London in 2012 at the ExCel Arena, whenever there were a couple of hours of a break in the boxing during the day I would spend it at weight-lifting, which attracted a crowd of ten thousand twice a day for the whole Olympics. I also went to watch table tennis and wrestling. I never missed a chance to go to other things and see other people.

You only have to be as good as you are at the time you are doing it: that is, you only have to push yourself within the confines of what you are up against. For instance, Herb Elliott is without doubt the greatest 1500-metres runner who ever lived. He never lost a race—and that includes all the major championships that were available to him. But his times wouldn't stand up now, though he won by a street at the time he was doing it.

Technology improves, with better shoes, which makes such a differ-ence, better conditioning, better nutrition, and better tracks. The tracks are incredibly different. Today's generation of athletes can focus solely on their goals, thanks to being sponsored, while previous generations had to go out and work to put food on the table.

You can bump into virtually anybody at the Olympics. We were at a dinner at the 1987 world championships and there was a call for the Bulgarian high-jumper Stefka Kostadinova. There was a window with a high sill on it, and she just stepped through the window! I've never seen the likes of it. I couldn't resist saying it to her when she came back, that I had never seen such legs as hers. She said something like, 'As long as that was all you were watching it was okay!'

On another occasion I was walking across a large footbridge in Sydney at the 2000 Games when suddenly a person came running past me at top speed and was hitting against people when running. He was obviously in an urgent hurry. I shouted: 'Where the feck are you running to? Who do you think you are—Sebastian Coe?' And sure who was it but Sebastian Coe!

Without further ado, here's my list of the most memorable—and some bizarre—moments of the Olympic Games.

NADIA COMĂNECI

I have seen a lot of iconic things during the eleven Summer Olympic Games I've attended so far. For instance, in 1976 I went to the gymnastics and I happened to be there the day the Romanian Nadia Comăneci made history by scoring the first perfect 10. Born in Moldavia, she was a doll, at 4 feet 11 inches. People said the Romanian doctors suppressed her sex organs when she was a child in order for her to be the optimum height and weight to win gold. But then when she left that programme, after moving to the United States, she grew up and became a normal-looking woman. Astonishing stuff!

She had been training to be a gymnast since the age of six. In Montreal she was fourteen years old and her greatest wish was to get on the various apparatus there, and she had planned and prayed that she was going to be in with a medal.

As it turned out she achieved the first perfect 10. Now, 9.9 would always have been given only if you were out of this world, but Nadia attained the perfect 10, which had never been done by a man or woman before. And because no-one had ever got 10 before, the electronic machine wasn't geared up for it, and they now had to work out how to convey a 10 to the public in the arena and the television audience. It seems funny now, with the way technology has advanced so much, but on this momentous occasion they couldn't put a 10 on the board! So the only thing they could do was put up the terribly low score of 1.0 and explain to the audience—who understood immediately—that she had received the perfect 10. But she also became the first gold-medallist ever to score just 1.0!

She went on to receive six more 10s on various apparatus in that Olympic Games. A few have got 10s since, but she got a rack of them.

STEVE REDGRAVE

I was at Sydney in 2000 when the British rower Steve Redgrave became the first person to win five gold medals at five consecutive Olympic Games. I'm not sure if Redgrave was any better than some of the others participating with him, but he was good enough over a sixteen-year period to win those five medals. You have to have luck to win so many medals consistently, but Redgrave—winner of nine world rowing championship gold medals—was also very good. It was amazing that he was able to maintain his form over that length of time in different types of boats and coaches. He was a pure gold-winner.

BOB BEAMON

I think the greatest feat in Olympic history in my time was back in 1968 when the American track and field athlete Bob Beamon broke the long-jump record. He did more than merely break the record in Mexico: he smashed it out of sight with a jump of 29 feet 2½ inches, which was an astonishing 22 inches better than the previous record, by the late great Jesse Owens, who had held that record for a quarter of a century.

Beamon achieved this fantastic incredible jump. There are great photographs of it, and they say he was six feet up in the air. Beamon bypassed 28 feet, which was amazing; and everyone at the time, including me, said this would last until the next century and maybe even beyond. But it was eventually broken, by a mere 2 inches, twenty-two years later, in 1991, by Mike Powell, who still holds the world record.

Beamon was so delighted with his result that he had what was called a cataleptic fit at the end of it: he went into a state of euphoria, which was like being knocked out, and even had to get medical attention.

It was said at the time that he had had sex the night before this almighty jump. Years after his famous record-breaking feat I was doing a programme called 'Champions' for RTE, and I jetted over to America to meet him at his house. I gingerly asked him if there was any truth in this story. He replied that he thought it was a bit funny that I'd be asking him such a question, but he went on to admit that it was indeed true. He told me when it was all over that he was worried that it would drain him and affect his game; but far from it!

ULRIKE MEYFARTH

I remember covering the 1972 Munich Games for radio when the West German high-jumper Ulrike Meyfarth made history by becoming the youngest athlete, at the age of sixteen, to win gold in that event. She made history again in 1984 when she won it a second time (not having won it in between) to become the *oldest* person to win the event, at the age of twenty-eight. She won it with an improvement of 4 inches from a world record of 63.5 inches to a new Olympic record of 67.5. Now that is some jump!

BEN JOHNSON

Another stand-out moment for me was seeing Ben Johnson live in action at Seoul in 1988. That was a big one! I was sitting in the canteen in the Olympic broadcast area when an American acquaintance of mine, who I hadn't seen in a few years, came over, and he told me there would be two really big stories from this particular Olympic Games; but he told me that he was sworn to secrecy, so he couldn't tell me what they were. He just told me to keep my eyes and ears open, and that one would be a male athlete and the other would be a female. 'They will blow the head of the whole Olympics,' he said.

I presumed the Canadian sprinter Ben Johnson was the male he was talking about, considering that he had already set the world record, though he then had all his medals—including the 1987 world championship medal—stripped from him for doping.

I felt they should have taken only the one medal where Johnson was found guilty of using banned substances. To be honest, I believe he probably was taking the stuff all right, but I don't think he was corrupt. I think the man who was looking after him was corrupt.

I felt it was wrong that he was stripped of his Olympic title that year and that everybody was promoted in the 100 metres, with Carl Lewis moving to gold, somebody else moved to silver, somebody else to bronze. One of them was Linford Christie, who has been highly suspect all along; but what can you do about these guys?

EDWIN MOSES

Edwin Moses just may be the best track and field sports star ever. The 400-metre hurdles was his speciality, and he won gold medals at the 1976 and 1984 Olympics Games. Sadly, he didn't get to compete in 1980 in Moscow, thanks to Jimmy Carter's decision to boycott the Games in Moscow during the so-called Cold War. If he had he certainly would have added more Olympic medals to his impressive cv.

Moses, who broke the world record on four occasions, also won the inaugural world championship in 1983 in Helsinki. He repeated this global feat in 1987 in Rome and again in 1991 in Tokyo. He went more than eighty races without a defeat. The cynics among you are probably wondering, 'Well, what was he on?' Let me tell you, Moses would probably give you a clatter if you made such an accusation to his face, because his career is stainless. Not alone that but he is now an anti-drugs campaigner with the International Olympic Committee. Moses, who I first got to know through the filming of the 'Superstars' show when he was participating in it, presented me with an award at the London Games in 2012 for having attended more than ten consecutive Olympic Games during my broadcasting career. It was a wonderful honour to receive my award from someone of his stature.

DICK FOSBURY

This very tall and impressive American (he was about 6 feet 5 inches) revolutionised the high jump when he introduced a unique so-called 'back first' technique in 1968, widely known today as the Fosbury flop, to clear the bar. It's a technique that is used by virtually every high-jumper since then: by 1980, thirteen of the sixteen high-jump finalists were doing the Fosbury flop. Before this revolutionary idea of curving backwards over the bar, the high-jumpers had used such techniques as the straddle, western roll, scissors-jump and eastern cut-off technique in order to land on their feet, because back in the good old days there wasn't any foam padding for the jumpers to land safely on—and nobody was going to jump backwards for fear of injuring themselves on hitting the sand or low matting surface.

I can still vividly recall watching in Mexico City as Fosbury raced to the high jump at great speed and took off with his left leg. The captivated crowd gasped when he didn't swing the next foot over but kept the right leg tucked under and then approached head-first, back to the bar. With this one small leap for mankind, the high jump was now in a new era, with no warning. It allowed Fosbury to clear every height up to 7 feet 4 inches and, in the process, win gold.

Along with Edwin Moses, Fosbury was one of a dozen celebrities who presented me with the Golden Flame replica in London in 2012 when I was being honoured for doing the commentary at more than ten Olympics. When he spoke to me at the London presentation in July 2012, I told him that he was the first Olympic champion to 'flop' and yet win! He said he liked that and was going to use it.

FRANCINA BLANKERS-KOEN, A.K.A. 'FLYING FANNY'

Flying Fanny went to the Olympic Games in Berlin in 1936 as an eighteen-year-old member of the Dutch team. She was so impressive all round that everyone said she would clean up at the next Olympics. Unfortunately for her, there were no next Games for eight years, as the Second World War was on in 1940 and also in 1944. The next Games were in 1948, but Fanny was still competing then, even though she was now thirty and the mother of two children. But that certainly didn't stop her from winning four—yes, count them—four gold medals in track and field: in the 100 metres, 200 metres, 80-metres hurdles, and relay. It made her the first woman to win four gold medals at the same Olympics Games.

When she was well into her eighties I interviewed her at her home, and she showed me all her medals. I had a picture taken with her and the medals. On another occasion when I interviewed her for a television show this elderly woman insisted on swimming for the camera to show how fit she was.

A truly wonderful woman, Fanny could do anything on the track: high jump, long jump . . . she was such an all-rounder. She was also the world record-holder in the long jump and high jump, in which she also competed in the Olympic Games. But she missed her best years, between the ages of twenty-two and twenty-six, as she was thirty when she won the four gold medals. Her records now don't seem to mean anything to the younger people reading them these days, but you must remember that in 1948 they didn't have the facilities or the beautiful tracks that they have now. I would nearly count her as number 1 sportswoman of all time.

JOHN AKII-BUA

The 400-metres hurdle is a speed glamour event. David Hemery of Great Britain was the 1968 champion, and he was the hot hurdles favourite in 1972 in Munich. He set an even faster pace, and I covered that race for television. He ran the first 200 metres in 22.8 and seemed certain to have a back-to-back Olympics; but what he wasn't counting on—well, none of us were counting on—was a man called John Akii-Bua from Uganda, who was on his way to a 47.82 world record. He was the first Olympic champion from his country. But John fell into the Idi Amin trap and he was jailed, then ended up as a refugee in Kenya before moving to Germany. He later went back home to coach. He is another man who disappeared: sadly, he died young, aged only forty-seven.

Chapter 4

MORE OLYMPIC STAND-OUT MOMENTS

J esse Owens was already a celebrity before he made history at the Berlin Olympics in 1936. He had made athletics history in Ann Arbor, Michigan, on 25 May 1935 when he set six world records in the span of forty-five minutes. But he became an international name after winning four gold medals in 1936, in the 100 metres, the 200 metres, the long jump, and the 4 × 100-metre relay team.

It was an uphill struggle for Owens to make his mark in track and field as the son of sharecroppers and the grandson of slaves. Growing up, teachers couldn't get his name right. When he was registering he said James Cleveland Owens, and they couldn't understand his accent, so he told them J. C. Owens, and that's what they called him, and that's how he became Jesse.

In Berlin in 1936—the much talked-about 'Hitler Games'—there is a story that Hitler snubbed Owens, but it's not true. Hitler was the master of the so-called Master Race, so one can only begin to imagine his reaction to the unthinkable prospect of a black man coming to Berlin, the home of the Third Reich, and running away with a handful of medals. It was said, and continues to be said, that the Führer got up off his seat when Owens was going for his fourth gold medal and walked out of the stadium. But that is not true. Yes, he did leave his seat at some point, but it wasn't during Owens's historic fourth win. You get a lot of stories like that.

Asked what was the secret of his success, Owens once said: 'I let my feet spend as little time on the ground as possible. From the air, fast down, and from the ground, fast up.' He didn't look over his shoulder either, to worry about who was stalking him on the track. He is probably the number 1 track and field athlete of all time.

Amazingly, he won all these gold medals while he was smoking a packet of cigarettes a day. Sadly, he died in March 1980 from lung cancer.

My father used to say to me, 'Ah, there'll never be another Jesse Owens.' But his Olympic record was replicated at the 1984 Games in Los Angeles by Carl Lewis, another athlete who deserved to be categorised as a *different class*. I was fortunate enough to be in the stadium to witness this historic moment at first hand, which has to be one of my favourite moments in any of the Olympics I've attended so far.

OLIVER KIRK

For my money, Oliver Kirk is entitled to be called the most remarkable of all Olympic boxing champions. He was certainly unique. In 1904, in St Louis, Missouri, this dazzling pugilist won both the bantamweight and the featherweight medals, and on the same day as well: 22 September 1904. He is also the only man to win two gold medals in the same Olympics in two different weight divisions. He did this by managing to lose 10 pounds to fight in the bantamweight.

JARMILA KRATOCHVÍLOVÁ

She may have won a silver medal at the 1980 Olympics, but this Czech athlete only really cemented her reputation as one of running's royalty when she not only won gold at the first world championship in Helsinki in 1983 but also broke world records in doing so. She was unmatchable at 400 and 800 metres; in fact her time of 1:53.28 in the 800 metres in July 1983 in Munich is still a record.

Kratochvílová seemed to be almost carved out of rock, from her shoulders, square, wide and prop-forwardish; her face was hardened by weather, and perhaps something else. Again there were whispers—correction, there were *shouts* of her being doped up to the eyeballs. It was never proved that she did take anything, so she deserves be in the *different class* category. But if Kratochvílová was taking anything, I'd bet she wouldn't have been the only woman athlete during those races taking illegal substances—essentially making it a level playing-field for those times.

Doping was the least of the Olympics' concerns back in the good old days, with even a sex test needed to investigate some of the dubious athletes. One of the most famous curious incidents was that of two Russian sisters, Irena and Tamara Press. They were practically built like rugby forwards—and I don't mean for women's teams but rather the Irish men's team. There were always people talking about them possibly being men, but nothing was ever proved. Yet when sex tests came in, in the mid-1970s, the Press sisters quickly disappeared, never to be seen again. Funnily enough, the only person who didn't have to do a sex test in 1976 was Princess Anne of Great Britain when she competed as a member of the British riding team!

Anyway, twenty years after Kratochvílová's famous victory I was returning from Madrid one day and I spotted a woman who looked quite like her. I mentioned this to Brian Moore of ITV, but he couldn't match this woman with her, and neither could Ron Pickering of the BBC, who did the racing commentary. Curiosity got the better of me, and I sidled over to her, and saw she was no longer so imposing. Her skin was now smooth: there was no sign of the bearded face! Making my apologies for confronting her, I asked her to tell me her name. 'Thank you for asking,' she replied. 'I am Jarmila Kratochvílová. Yes, I was a world champion in 1983.'

She was a most pleasant person, and it would be hard to find a nicer encounter. If she had been on something else she had obviously quit it by this stage!

EMIL ZÁTOPEK

This Czech long-distance runner won gold in London in 1948, but his greatest success was in Helsinki in 1952, where, incredibly, he won three gold medals: in the 5,000 metres, the 10,000 metres, and the marathon. It's something unique that has never been achieved by anybody since. When he won the 5,000 metres his wife, Dana, won the discus on the very same afternoon. And they were both born on the same day!

On top of his four Olympic gold and one silver medal he won three gold medals and one bronze at the European Athletics Championships.

He also holds the distinction of making a world record when he broke the 29-minute barrier in the 10k back in 1954. He was so good, in fact, that the magazine *Runner's World* selected him as the greatest runner of all time.

TEÓFILO (FILO) STEVENSON

Up until 1972 the big star of the Olympics in number of medals was the Hungarian boxer László Papp, the only man ever to win three Olympic medals. But that record was matched in 1972 by a Cuban. Cuba was beginning to make its presence felt in world boxing and in world sport in general. At the 1972 Olympics they had a heavyweight called Teófilo Stevenson, who was a massive puncher, beautiful and stylish. He was a good-looking man and he was definitely a poster boy, but he wasn't in the Cuban team for those reasons: he was just a fantastic boxer.

I first saw him in action in Munich when I was doing the boxing commentary there. So I saw him a lot and I knew he would go all the way, despite the Americans thinking they had the gold medal sewn up. They had a contract for Duane Bobick for a million dollars when he won the Olympics—not *if* he won, *when* he won. Well, he finally met Stevenson, who took him apart, really, and put him out and down; and the big dream of the Americans was gone. He blew them out of the water.

Stevenson went on to the final of the Olympics in 1972, where his Romanian opponent couldn't carry on because he was injured. Whether he was injured was another story; like many of us at the time I said to myself, 'I wonder is he actually injured? Or is discretion the better part of valour?' Anyway, Stevenson was one of the stars of the Olympics in 1972.

In 1976 we went to Montreal, and Stevenson was even better there and cleaned up all around him at the Olympics.

He went to Moscow in 1980, when President Carter blocked the Americans from competing in it. Stevenson was probably at his very best, and he won the Olympics again. He wouldn't have been able to go to Los Angeles, because the Cubans and the other communist countries came back at the USA over the Carter ban and boycotted the Olympics in the United States.

I got to meet him in America, in Reno, Nevada, when the world championships were held there in the 1980s, and I remember the American journalists all lined up asking him things—it was at the time that the USA-Cuba thing was hot—and they were questioning him about it. Stevenson knew his facts and figures, and he said: 'Before the time of Fidel Castro, Cuba had won nothing. Since Castro took over Cuba has won.' I'm not going to pretend to remember all he said, but he had his facts right and was able to say they won 193 gold medals, 193 silver medals, etc. He knew it all, and it was really a pro-Castro speech. He was the brightest of the bright. He was a great champion.

VASILY ALEKSEYEV

When it comes to weightlifting, the Russian Vasily Alekseyev is up there as one of the all-time greats—if not the greatest—with his record of two gold medals at the Olympics, coupled with eight gold medals at the World Weightlifting Championship and a further eight gold medals at the European Championships. I think he holds the record for winning the most Russian titles too. He also broke more than eighty world records. He was nearly a world record himself with his sheer size, because he weighed 24 stone 10 pounds when he was only thirty-four years old!

He was unbeaten for twelve years, and he was paid a thousand dollars by the Soviet government every time he broke a world record, which he seemed to do every three to four times per year. He was a sight to behold!

I never saw such a mighty crowd at a weightlifting event as at Montreal in 1976. I went to the venue one evening so I might see this mighty Soviet lifter, who made 440 kilos in total weight, and that included 255 in a clean and jerk.

Although I was fully accredited for the Games, I found that access was impossible because there was a huge queue to get in. I was queuing for forty-five minutes, which is unheard of for the press. With the clock ticking, it took an exhibition of blarney to convince the stewards and the security that my presence was absolutely essential for the career well-being of the Russian!

BLACK POWER

It was at the height of the Black Power thing in America, and they had supporters in at least two American athletes, who were first and third in the 200 metres. They were two of the best athletes in every sense: Tommie Smith and John Carlos. When they were on the podium getting their medals they decided (obviously prearranged) that they would give the Black Power salute. They were supposed to have gloves on, but they only had one pair, so Tommie Smith wore one on his right hand and John Carlos wore the other one on his left hand. It was the beginning of this entire grass-roots campaign in America. They were taken out of their quarters in the Olympic Village by the American authorities and sent home. It was a big so-called sin to commit. That was before the death of Martin Luther King and all that. It was both a stupid and also a courageous thing to do, I think.

THE NEARLY MAN: THE 1972 MEN'S MARATHON

I was covering this famous race. They were coming near the close in the stadium, and the first fella appears after running 26 miles, and of course the crowd rise to him and give him a great, great reception. I didn't know who he was, and I said so, which was some admission to make live on air! And sure it turned out I was right. When he was half way around the track or more, Frank Shorter of America appeared in the stadium, and he was the real leader. It turned out that this guy was an impostor, a West German student named Norbert Sudhaus, who had decided to jump into the end of the race for a joke. It was far from funny.

By now the crowd had begun booing the impostor, and security men came to remove him from the track. But when poor old Shorter arrived, he was welcomed by a storm of hissing. He couldn't understand why they were booing when he had done nothing wrong and he was about to win the gold medal. It did take away his moment of glory in winning, but he was the real winner. It's quite rare for a winner to be booed at the finishing line!

STRANGE OLYMPIC BOXING STORIES

It must be one of the oddest fights in history when the famous Swedish boxer Ingemar Johansson was in the heavyweight final in 1952 and he didn't make an attempt to box against a fella called Ed Sanders. The referee tried to encourage them to box, and he didn't, as he wasn't too keen on it; and eventually in round 2 the referee stopped the contest and awarded it to Sanders, and Johansson was disqualified for 'passivity', which was on the official report.

People who were anti-Johansson said he was afraid of Sanders, who had knocked out everyone he had boxed against the previous year. Maybe he was, but he himself said he thought Sanders was waiting for him to attack, and he was waiting for Sanders to catch him on the counter-attack. They didn't give him his silver medal until thirty years later, in 1981.

Another unusual boxing event was when Evander Holyfield, who later became world heavyweight champion, met a guy called Kevin Barry from New Zealand in the 1984 Olympics. The referee called 'break'. The referee in amateur boxing only says three words— everything else is body language: he says 'Break,' 'Stop,' and 'Box.' On the call of 'break' in the tussle between these two, Holyfield was in the process of letting a punch go, and it caught Barry and knocked him out, and he was counted out. Holyfield was disqualified for punching after the instruction, and Barry couldn't fight in the final; until a certain number of days after a knock-out you are not medically allowed to box. So neither of them fought in the final, and it was a walkover for Josipović of Yugoslavia. It was an unusual thing in that Holyfield then won the world title, and that, from an Irish point of view, it was a man called Kevin Barry at the heart of it all.

I also remember an incident in the boxing at the Seoul 1988 Olympics. I was only yards away from the action. There was a Korean boxer called Byun Jung-Il, and he was fighting a guy called Hristov from Bulgaria, and it was a rough enough contest. The Korean was cautioned by the referee a couple of times, and eventually he warned him again—and a warning is a point away to your opponent, and the second warning is two points to the opponent. So by doing that he swung the balance to his opponent, and Hristov won it.

There was then a massive row. The Korean coach jumped into the ring and hit the referee, a New Zealander called Keith Walker. He stumbled forward, and the next fella got into the ring, and it was obvious there was something serious about to happen. I ended up ducking as they started throwing chairs and stuff at each other.

A fella did one of these spectacular kung fu-type of moves on a man called Emil Jetchev, who was chairman of the referee judges committee, who they reckoned had something to do with it. He just took off, ducking to get out of the way of the flying kung-fu kick. I don't know how he managed to do it, as I could see it clearly, but he ducked at the last second, and your man went whizzing by him and went flying into the partition ahead of me, and I heard a loud crack. It nearly killed him stone dead.

During the fracas the security people came in and grabbed the referee and hustled him out of the place to the airport, and they flew him to London. In the meantime Byun sat in the ring in protest at not getting the decision. He was given a whole lot of warnings to get out and he ignored them. Time went by, about forty-five minutes, and he was still there, and they eventually got him a chair. He sat down on the chair, and then they put out the lights, turned off all the gear, while he kept sitting there, for a total of one hour and seven minutes—to break the record of protest at an Olympic event. The previous record was actually held by another Korean boxer, in 1964. Byun didn't deserve to win, so he was just being thick.

THE FUNNIEST MOMENT

The International Olympic Committee decided in their infinite wisdom that they would invite some athletes from poorer countries (in the sense of poorer in sporting achievement) to the Sydney Games in 2000, I think. Three of them were in the 100-metres swimming heat. They had one heat of the 100-metres with these three guys in it: a fella from Niger called Bare and a guy called Oripov from Tajikistan and a guy called Eric Moussanbani from Equatorial Guinea. And they were standing on the starting-blocks, and the two boys jumped into the water in anticipation and were disqualified, which left only one in the heat, and that was Moussanbani. The starting-gun went, and off he went up the pool, struggling. The only swimming he had ever done in preparation for this had been in the hotel swimming-pool in Equatorial Guinea!

When he got to the top of the pool he just couldn't hack it at all. The crowd were trying to help him by shouting out words of encouragement. He stopped kind of half way, and he just couldn't make it, because he just wasn't really a swimmer. But the crowd kept urging him on. Really, you could say that the crowd dragged him to the finish in the end, which was an achievement in itself. For the 100-metre freestyle he took 1 minute 52.72 seconds, which is nearly a minute slower than the normal winner.

Journalists called him Eric the Eel; it came in the wake of Eddie the Eagle, the guy doing the ski-jumping, and he was just brutal at it. In fact he couldn't do it at all, but he just entered the Winter Olympics for some bizarre unknown reason. I suppose there's one born every minute, as the saying goes.

MARY PETERS

It was the pentathlon rather than the heptathlon! In 1972 Mary Peters stole the show on day 2 of the women's multi-event in track and field. The 33-year-old Belfast woman wasn't expected to beat the local German, Heidi Rosendahl, as she was the long-jump specialist. There was one segment remaining, and that was the 200 metres, in which each woman ran her personal best. Peters clocked 48.01 and Rosendahl 47.91, and when everything was translated into points Peters had a new world record, of 4,801 points, to win by just 10 points from the German. Had Peters run that final 200 metres a tenth of a second slower she would not have won the gold medal in Munich 1972.

ZOLA BUDD

The South African Zola Budd was an amazing runner who achieved fame at the age of seventeen when she broke the women's 5,000-metre world record. But the International Amateur Athletic Federation refused to recognise it as a record, because at the time South Africa was excluded from international competitions because of apartheid. She made such a cultural impact in her native South Africa that township taxis there today are called Zola Budd, because of their speed.

So, because she was denied access to the big-time sports meetings she opted to run for Britain, as her grandmother was from there; it was one of those 'Does your mother come from Ireland?' type of things like in the Jack Charlton era.

After she got classification for the British team Zola entered the 3,000 metres in Los Angeles. While she never won a medal at the Olympics, she was involved in one of its most infamous races. In fact she would have won a medal only that, as she later claimed in her autobiography, she slowed down in order not to win, because she couldn't bear the thought of facing a hostile home crowd after colliding with the local hero, Mary Decker—or Little Miss Decker, as they called her in America.

Decker was a tiny little woman who had first come on the scene in 1973, an American icon, who had won two gold medals at the inaugural world championship in Helsinki in 1983. She went on the strength of this to Los Angeles in 1984 as a cast-iron certainty; but what happened to her was over the top. I was doing commentary on the race, and there were 85,000 people in the Coliseum. Decker was the red-hot favourite.

It all began when Decker clipped Budd's heels. Budd was just ahead of Decker, and to the best of my knowledge Decker clipped Budd's heel and knocked her slightly off balance; but both women continued running. Shortly afterwards they made contact again when Budd's foot tipped Decker's thigh, which caused the South African to fall into Decker's path. But the American's spiked shoes came down on Zola's ankle. Decker fell into the infield and lay there crying, through bad humour, injury and disappointment. There was no healing the American, who lay there crying and whingeing.

Yet despite drawing blood, despite the pain, Zola continued and was in first place for a while, until she purposely slowed down, as she claims in her autobiography. Zola finished down the field, somewhere around seventh place, and the race was won by Maricica Puică of Romania. Nobody had counted on Puică—despite the fact that she had broken a world record that year.

Afterwards a very contrite Zola was in the area where athletes assemble, and she was trying to pacify Decker. She apologised and did everything, but Decker wouldn't have any of it, and she told her in unconventional language to get lost. Zola went back to her again, but Decker refused to talk to her. It certainly showed Decker in a different light from the image of the beautiful all-American sweetheart athlete.

Poor old Zola! This incident really ended her career, because she felt she wasn't wanted in the big bad world. And we didn't see much of Decker after that either. It was an easy one for the commentators, because neither of them won a damn thing of any real significance after that disaster. If Zola had just kept going she would have won gold, or silver at the very least; but today she's remembered only for that unfortunate clash.

WILMA RUDOLPH

I was sitting one day in the restaurant of a hotel in Barcelona when I noticed a woman who was having lunch at an adjacent table with another woman. I knew that I knew her. So, cheekily, I went over to her and identified myself and said, 'I think I know who you are. Are you Wilma?' And she said yes, she was. It was Wilma Rudolph, a fantastic sprinter who won three gold medals in the 100, 200 and relay in the 1960 Olympics. She won a bronze that year too.

She was the registrar in a hospital in Nashville, Tennessee, so we talked about Nashville and country music and all the rest of it. We spoke about her upbringing. She had polio, which affected her greatly until she was eleven, and she had to have the callipers on her legs and all. She then had to have an operation to get her legs right. Yet despite this horrible ordeal she managed to become the fastest woman on earth. To me that was one of the best days I have ever had: meeting this woman who faced such adversity and made history. Sadly, she died only two years after our brief meeting.

LASSE VIRÉN

This Finnish policeman won four consecutive gold medals as a long-distance runner in the 1972 and 1976 Olympics, in both the 5,000 and 10,000-metre events.

He began his medal collection on 31 August 1972 in the Munich Olympic stadium. David Bedford, a famous English runner, had set a cracking pace and at 4,600 metres in the 10,000 metres seemed to be the winner. But all the drama was happening behind him. Virén was running in fifth place, and he began to stumble. He didn't seem to hit anyone: he just stumbled, and then fell into the infield. With that the Moroccan runner tripped over him. Virén got up quickly and began chasing after the others. When they went into the last 800 metres the Finn showed his unbelievable class: he ran the second-last lap in 60 seconds and the last in 56.4 seconds to catch up and to win. It's an almost unbelievable event, thinking about it now.

Ron Clarke had held the world record for seven years up until then, but his record was just wiped off the boards, making a new world record for the Finn of 27 minutes 43.28 seconds.

On that day in 1972 Virén had won the first of his four gold medals, and he accomplished the 5,000-metre and 10,000-metre double in Munich and replicated the distance double in Montreal in 1976. Funnily enough, the silver medal in the 1976 10,000-metre race went to a man from Portugal called Carlos Lopes, who got the gold medal when John Treacy won the silver in Los Angeles in 1984 in the marathon. But that's a different story.

Chapter 5 ∾

|THE BEAUTIFUL GAME

A s the old saying goes, if I had a pound for every time I was asked who my all-time soccer team is I'd be on the proverbial pig's back.

You could argue until Doomsday about who are the greatest eleven players, but for my money I'd have in goal either the Great Dane, Peter Schmeichel, who was voted the best goalkeeper in the world at the height of his career with Manchester United, or the Irishman Pat Jennings, who became the first player in English football to reach a thousand senior appearances during a stellar career with Spurs and Arsenal. I'd probably have to toss a coin to decide which one would make the cut in my fantasy team. I'd have Paolo Maldini, who played with AC Milan until he was forty-one, at either left back or in the centre. The Italian, nicknamed Il Capitano, has the distinction of being the first defender to win *World Soccer's* annual World Player of the Year award. It was a well-deserved accolade, which the man himself said was 'a particular matter of pride, because defenders generally receive so much less attention from fans and the media than goal-scorers. We are more in the engine room rather than taking the glory.' At right back I would select Carlos Alberto Torres. He was outstanding in the 1970 World Cup when he captained Brazil to victory. Pelé once named him as one of the greatest players ever.

Franz Beckenbauer, dubbed Der Kaiser, stood out for Germany in the 1974 World Cup victory over the Dutch. It would be hard not to include such a magnificent defender, generally regarded as the greatest German player of all time.

I make no apologies, but at second centre back I would opt for the great Paul McGrath. He'd make Beckenbauer twice as good. (I'll discuss in more detail later, in the chapter on Irish soccer, why McGrath was truly a *different class*.)

In midfield I'd have no hesitation in opting for Johan Cruyff, who was not only voted European Player of the Century by the International Federation of Football History and Statistics but came second in their poll behind Pelé for their World Player of the Century. No mean feat! In my opinion John Giles would have to be seriously considered to partner Cruyff in midfield, as the former Irish captain and manager could run the whole show if he wanted. I'd also probably have to find a place for George Best, perhaps on one wing, and either Cristiano Ronaldo or Messi—my God, what a player he is!—on the other wing.

Another question I'm always asked is, 'Who's better, Messi or Ronaldo?' Again, it's a hard one to answer, as both, for me, are as good as one another. Again, you could flip a coin.

Up front I'd pair Pelé with Maradona. It would be hard to imagine such a line-up ever losing a match!

Unfortunately I can only pick eleven players. But one that would give the aforementioned a run for their money is Stanley Matthews, who was also an astonishing player. I had the privilege of meeting him in Malta some time back in the early 1970s. He was Sir Stanley Matthews by this stage—making him the first footballer to be knighted. When I discovered that he was in Malta I made it my business to try and seek him out. I made contact with a friend of mine who was able to organise it for me. I was only a youngfella starting out in broadcasting at the time and I was in awe of Matthews. In my childhood he was simply the best. He was one of the fellas that I used to write to as a child, asking them how they used to play their game; I'd ask questions like, 'How do you switch your balance from left to right?' etc. You couldn't pick up a paper at the time without Matthews being mentioned in it. He had several nicknames, all entirely apt: the Wingman of Wizardry, the Magician, and the Wizard of Dribble.

He began his career playing with Stoke, and then he went to Blackpool, with whom he won the FA Cup in 1953—when he was forty years old, to boot! That was also the last time Blackpool won the FA cup. After this he went back to Stoke, who were then in the now defunct First Division, and he continued to play for them until he was fifty-one. It wasn't a token experience, as he played a number of times that year. He's probably the only player to be still going strong at the very top at such an age. It's an astonishing feat when you think about it.

He played for England throughout four decades too: the 1930s, 40s, 50s and 60s. Sadly, he never won the League. In those days you mostly played for your local team, and there wasn't the huge money involved that there is now. It's hard to rate Matthews and put him in a list of top British players. I find myself thinking, 'Sure I wouldn't have him at number 1 anyway!' And then I'd ask myself, 'Why wouldn't you?' There's no denying that he would be perhaps the most entertaining British player but, if you're a full-back, also the most annoying. Matthews would be the dribbling genius of football; he played outside on the right and would without fail always bamboozle the full-backs, taking the best and making them dizzy. 'Almost no-one could stop him,' Franz Beckenbauer once observed.

When we met in Malta I said to him, 'This record of yours will never be beaten, playing in the First Division at fifty-one years of age. Have you any regrets?'

He replied without hesitating: 'Yes. I retired too soon!'

I found myself laughing at this comment.

'It's true. I was every bit as good when I was fifty as I was when I was forty,' he insisted.

I believed him too. I don't believe in this ageism thing at all. I will never forget that statement. He was close to sixty then but still remarkably fit. He was still match-fit.

———

It goes without saying that the Olympics is my favourite sports event, but the FIFA World Cup is a close second. It all began on 13 July 1930 in Montevideo when thirteen countries entered and played in it, including Brazil, who have never missed any World Cup finals. They will definitely be in the next one, as they are hosting it. These thirteen countries assembled in the Uruguayan capital, and the home country became the first world champions. Football has since become one of the biggest crowd-pullers in all sport; it's the best for stadium attendance figures, and of course the television audience is immense, with countless millions of people tuning in every four years to watch it.

This assembly of nations is terrific. FIFA has 210 members, which is, astonishingly, more than the United Nations—and nearly all enter, unless they are banned for some reason, such as non-payment of dues, and compete to qualify for the finals. When you get to the final itself it's special, because no tournament in sport can match it for colour and drama . . . hats, furs, badges. There is a big market in the badges: you need to bring a collection of Irish badges with you when you are travelling, as people are always wanting to swap them. A lot of the countries, particularly African countries, dress in their national dress, which is lovely to observe.

I really think every World Cup is big. I went to my first World Cup in 1966 and did some work for RTE radio. I have worked at them all since 1966—more than a dozen tournaments in total—and I have been at every final since 1966.

I suppose most people would probably argue that the 1974 tournament—the first one without the Jules Rimet Trophy, which was replaced by the FIFA World Cup, designed by the Italian sculptor Silvio Gazzaniga—was perhaps the most memorable, because at that time the Netherlands had a wonderful team. It would be fair to say they were the people's champions, because they played beautiful football, so-called total football, and people wanted that sort of football to win. But that year's winners, Germany, it has to be said, were also brilliant.

For me, however, the stand-out World Cup is probably either of the ones held in Mexico in 1970 or 1986. The stand-out moment for me is always any time Brazil takes to the field. But the 1986 tournament will always be remembered for Maradona. Yes, I totally agree that Argentina didn't have a great team, but they always had Maradona. Brazil are always brilliant, but I'll never forget how their first of five World Cups in 1958 was won with a certain seventeen-year-old boy playing for them. Unbelievable! When Pelé came on the scene, in 1958, Brazil won their first World Cup, and by the time he left the scene, in 1970, they had won three of their four World Cups, which elevates Pelé above everyone, in my estimation.

I remember Pelé being kicked out of the World Cup in Liverpool in 1966 by Portugal. He was literally kicked out, as they took it in turns to foul him. He was eventually taken off, hobbling and crying, and he said that was the end of World Cups for him; but luckily enough he changed his mind and came back in 1970 at his very best. In that Portuguese team I must emphasise that Eusébio, who at the time they were saying was the new Pelé, did *not* cheat. There is always a new somebody, according to the hype.

Brazil had wonderful squads during those times, with Pelé on form, but the 1970 squad was a particularly breathtaking team, with Carlos Alberto, Tostão—who is often described as one of the best forwards— and Jairzinho, who scored in every game in that tournament. A great team—perhaps even the best team ever to win it.

Speaking of Pelé, I was recently visiting the Children's Hospital in Tallaght, which is the oldest children's hospital in Ireland, to present awards for raising money. Funnily enough, they are now twinned with a hospital in Brazil for facilities, doctors, medicines etc. and they presented me with a Pelé Peace Medal.

Another great thing about the World Cup is that you get to travel. In South Africa I went to Johannesburg, Durban, Cape Town; in Spain I went to Barcelona, Madrid, Valencia. I personally (and I wasn't the only one) did more travel in the first five days of the US '94 World Cup than an airline steward! I went from Dallas to Los Angeles to San Francisco to Washington and back to Dallas.

Another thing I remember about that World Cup was Diana Ross doing a celebrity kick-off to officially open the World Cup. It was the shortest kick-off ever, because she literally couldn't move the ball! It moved at most two inches. She may have been Diana Ross of the Supremes, but there was nothing supreme about that kick!

Apart from the travelling, another great thing about the World Cup is the number of legendary figures I've been fortunate enough to meet, such as the brilliant di Stéfano, who once played in a friendly match I organised with Bobby Charlton; Ferenc Puskás, who is also widely regarded as one of the all-time great players; Francisco Gento of Real Madrid; Denis Law; Just Fontaine, who holds the record for scoring most goals in a single World Cup, with thirteen at the 1958 tournament for France; Eusébio; Pelé; Mazzola; Bobby and Jack Charlton. At World Cup events you'd be able to find them all in the one room, chatting away about who is the greatest. It can be a real pinch-yourself moment, though after a while you do get used to seeing your idols.

It's fantastic seeing so many countries, experiencing so many different cultures, so many languages. It's brilliant when it works; but it hasn't always worked.

Here's an example of when it turned into a nightmare. In 1986 in Mexico I was doing the first Brazil match for television. There were forty-three countries taking part, and there was mayhem, because countries didn't get their live feed, with others getting feeds in the wrong language. But luckily we at RTE got our feed. The technicians from various stations were frantically carrying out tests, and I immediately smelt trouble on the horizon and heard all these big loud voices and saw all the fellas pulling their hair out when they realised that the feeds were linked up incorrectly. You had the likes of the Swedish station getting audio meant for Saudi Arabia, and vice versa. It was a complete mix-up.

At a meeting the next day the Europeans were very annoyed about the amount of money spent and the preparations involved, etc., and saying that they should take the Mexicans to court. The leader of the Irish delegation said: 'What a good idea that is! Because the Mexican government at this moment only owes us 135 million dollars. So I would say they would be really frightened of a case against them.' So that defused the whole thing!

I remember one funny episode during that particular World Cup. Brazil were playing, and you have the Brazilian nicknames, like Pelé, rather than his full name of Edison Arantes do Nascimento, which would certainly be more than a mouthful if you had to say it when doing the commentary on a match. Luckily enough, all the Brazilians have nicknames; but on this occasion, when the team sheets were handed out they had their official full names, and nobody in the Irish media contingent seemed to know who they were. Panicking, they were all practically turning to me, frantically asking, 'Who's this Brazilian player, Jimmy?' The place was in turmoil.

I remember Ray Treacy was doing the colour piece, and he said, 'Ha, Maestro, there's one for you.' Perhaps he didn't think I'd know them all, but I replied: 'Don't be worrying. You know all these men: that there is Dirceu, that's Edu, that's Jairzinho.' As it turned out, for once I did something right!

All the World Cups are of a *different class*, but some of them are elevated to that status by the appearance of some special players, like Pelé, Eusébio and Maradona, who it appeared to almost single-handedly make the '86 World Cup special.

Chapter 6 ～

| AMONG THE BEST

I often get asked, 'Who is the best you have ever seen play Gaelic football and hurling?' I always kind of shy away from answering it, because as far as I'm concerned there really is no way of saying there is only one best, no more than you can say what the best song you ever heard is.

However, you can say 'among the best.' And if you are talking about Gaelic football one of the most skilful and maybe one of the best, if not *the* best, was Jack O'Shea. The Kerryman was a great all-rounder for a midfielder; he was a great catcher, a great kicker, a great runner, and maybe the best long-kicker I have ever seen. He had what seemed like inexhaustible energy, running up and down the field. He scored a few great goals in Croke Park, and he should have been chosen for the Millennium Team, but for some inexplicable reason he wasn't selected. He was certainly robbed there.

I scratch my head when I think about how he didn't even make the Hall of Fame either. The first fifteen players inducted into the Gaelic Hall of Fame are the exact same fifteen players who are on the Millennium Team, which was a sensible way, I suppose, but it meant Jack didn't make the cut.

I asked a lot of footballers over the years, 'Who would you say is among the best ever?' No matter who I have asked, Jack O'Shea is always mentioned. He is always in the top five and most often named as their number 1. He played with me in the All-Stars, which I set up to play matches around the country for charity. So I know what he was capable of. Naturally these charity games I organised weren't high-profile games or competitive games, but you could still see him doing things like catching a ball over everyone's head and kicking it seventy yards accurately. To be able to do that is just mighty.

He still loves the game. You can see him at games regularly. Kerry is a bit like Brazil in football terms, because they are the number 1 team, with something like thirty-six All-Ireland wins, and Jack has seven himself, which is not a bad percentage. Seven out of thirty-six championships means he has won almost a fifth of Kerry's All-Ireland finals.

Jack always reminded me of Pat Spillane, who was out of this world as a fantastic player, with great energy. But if I had to pick my second-favourite player I would opt for the legendary Christy Ring, the champion Cork hurler.

I first met Christy in Hartford, Connecticut. He was essentially a shy man; he did his talking with his stick. He was a non-drinker, and it was after I gave up booze for good back in 1973; but we two non-drinkers first met in a bar one night. We got talking about his career and everything. He told me the other great player of his time was Mick Mackey. People used to ask who was better, Ring or Mackey—one of those things that people do. So I asked Ring about it.

'Ah, yeah, Mackey was fantastic,' he told me. 'I remember one day we were playing and we were both captains, and the referee tossed the coin. And if you're captain of a team you must know what the strengths of your team are.

'So, it came down on heads, and without thinking I said, "We will play that way." And Mackey said, "Oh, no, you won't!" Because he won the toss, he said, "We will play that way."'

Laughing, he said to me, 'That's the way I wanted to play in the first place!' He had tricked him. Ring was cute, and he admitted it himself.

He told me about another time playing in a Cork club match for Glen Rovers against UCC. He recalled: 'I had this reputation'—he wasn't shy about saying he had a reputation, but he wasn't big-headed either—'for being fearless, and I got a little nick—no more than a shaving cut. I got the blood and I rubbed it around my face, and I got the ball and ran straight for the goal. I swear the goalkeeper stood out of my way, and I buried it in the net. That's what you get for being cute!'

Christy played in the All-Stars for me and came on our American tour back in the '70s. We were in Hartford, Connecticut, one day, and we were playing in a country field, rather than a stadium, that was just outside the city limits. We were playing against a New York and Hartford selection. Before our game there was a softball game on, and the lads decided that Christy would be good at it and wanted him to have a go. Christy wasn't to be found, because he was away off the far side of the field, hiding behind a tree but watching the game. One of the lads said, 'Sure he'll come over for *you*, Jimmy.'

I toddled over to Christy. 'The lads want you to have a go at this softball, Christy.'

'Do *you* want me to have a go at it?'

'Yes, Christy.'

'All right so.'

And we went back over.

'Give me that what-do-you-call-it,' he said, knowing damn well what it's called. 'Is that a bat or a stick, or what do you call it?'

'A bat.'

'All right, thank you. Now, do you hold it like that or do you hold it like this?'

They were all questions he knew the answers to, because he had been watching the game. Then he said, 'Now, who's your best pitcher?'

'Billy Kyle Junior.'

So Christy asked them to bring Billy Kyle out. This youngfella of about nineteen came out and pitched for an underhand softball, and Christy hit it, and it went over the wall and down the highway. It kept going until it was out of sight.

'That's a home run, now, isn't it?' Christy said, and then threw down the bat and nonchalantly walked away. That's the kind of man he was: he was only interested in perfection. Late in life he took up squash and became Munster champion, never having played the game before.

Very often he would ask you leading questions, such as, 'You were good on Saturday.'

'Thanks, Christy.'

'Who was the best player on the field?'

There's no definitive answer to that, is there, unless it's Ronaldo or

Pelé! 'Well, I suppose, taking everything into account, Lindsay in defence.'

'You're a man who knows something about it,' he would reply, which meant that he agreed with me. And then he would go through the whole rigmarole of why that man was the best: 'Because he stepped there when the ball was there. He would be out of place when the ball was there,' etc., etc.

Christy was a winner all the way. He loved winning, and he knew how to win. We used a roll-on, roll-off system, and I was playing on the field and he would say to me, 'Did you find it yet, Jimmy?'

'What's that, Christy?'

'The thing you're looking for, Jimmy. You're running around the same spot, Jimmy. You haven't moved out of it.' That was his way of getting at me because I was standing in the same spot. 'Did you lose your contact lenses?'

'No, Christy.'

'Well, let me out there and I'll have a look for you.'

So I would go off and he would come on. God, he went mad and scored a goal and a couple of points and then went back off again. You couldn't tire him out; at this stage he was in his fifties, but Christy was a very, very special person. Sadly, he died only eight years after this trip to the States. He was a genius of a man.

I saw him shortly before he died, because he was still involved in the Jimmy Magee All-Stars with me at the time. He was quite a funny man and very forthcoming. He died a relatively young man, only sixty years old. He just dropped dead. You would never even have thought that he would go. The former Taoiseach Jack Lynch spoke at the graveside. Lynch was his team-mate in Cork, and he said, 'So long as young men play hurling, and so long as people talk about the game, the name of Christy Ring will be remembered for ever.'

Christy was good to me. He never shied away from me; he always gave me an interview and spoke to me. I think it was because he knew I was genuinely passionate about sport. Everyone in Ireland would say, Christy is the number 1 hurler of all time, and I would agree; but there are so many great all-timers coming along now, like D. J. Carey, Eddie Keher and Henry Shefflin.

Shefflin has outscored everybody in his career, including Eddie Keher, D. J. Carey and, even more remarkably, Christy Ring. He is the top scorer of all time. Ring was a magical figure and was a crowd-puller. If I had to choose between the two I would have to opt for Ring, but I would prefer to have the two of them on my side.

———

I have some special memories of GAA, both football and hurling. Perhaps one of the greatest goals I ever saw was by Séamus Darby in 1982, when Kerry were going for their famous five in a row. It was the age of the great Kerry team. Darby was a sub on the bench for Offaly, and when they eventually brought him on he got the ball and scored the goal to prevent Kerry from winning the Sam Maguire Cup. Those who were on the negative side said he pushed Tommy Doyle; those on the positive side said he didn't; and those who were telling the truth didn't tell it! Tommy Doyle himself has no axe to grind. Darby got it, and a bullet of a shot on the Fairview end of the ground, and Kerry lost it in the dying minutes.

I was there when Down first won it in 1960 and therefore became the first county to bring the Sam Maguire Cup across the border. I was there in 1957 when the showband star Dermot O'Brien, who just happened to be a very good friend of mine, led Louth to victory in the All-Ireland. He went that morning to the Bon Secours Hospital in Glasnevin for some attention to an injury he had and to make sure he could play. When he got back to the ground he couldn't get into the stadium and he had to plead to get in, and somebody eventually recognised him as the captain of Louth and let him in!

When he got in and went over to the Louth dressing-room the rest were standing there ready to go out onto the field, and somebody said, 'Here's Dermo, throw a jersey on there.' He didn't even have time to tie his bootlaces.

I saw the great Kerry-Dublin rivalry develop and take shape and produce some of the greatest players and games ever seen. Dublin had great players, such as Brian Mullins, Jimmy Keaveney, Kevin Moran and Bernard Brogan, whose two sons are now on the Dublin team. For Kerry, of course, you had the three Spillanes, Michael, Pat and Tom, as well as Mikey Sheehy and the wonderful Jack O'Shea. I saw Mick O'Connell in his prime. These guys made the game exciting.

There was a very good spell of Ulster supremacy that kind of coincided with Peter Quinn from Fermanagh being president of the GAA. In 1991 Down won the All-Ireland; then in 1992 Donegal won the All-Ireland, and then it was Derry's turn in 1993, and Down again in 1994. Think about it: three different Northern counties in four consecutive years. It was a fantastic time for Ulster. Donegal in 1992 was the last time, and the only time they won it, until 2012. And that first goal they got in 2012 by Michael Murphy was one of the greatest goals ever scored in an All-Ireland final. They certainly have some of the best players, and they even wrote songs about their manager, Jim McGuinness.

Peter Canavan of Tyrone deserves a special mention. I don't think there was ever a man with his weight and size as good in the history of the game. Seán O'Neill from Down was a mighty man; and Maurice Fitzgerald from Kerry.

These are all footballers. With regard to hurlers, Kilkenny had a drove of them, like Henry Shefflin, D. J. Carey, and Eddie Keher; for Cork, Jimmy Barry Murphy, John Hartnett, John Fenton. With Tipperary you had all the Ryans, Nicholas English, and all the Bonnars. They were wonderful times to be a follower of GAA and not a specific team, because I don't really support anyone, bar myself, and I find it hard enough to do that!

The last time my own county, Louth, was nearly there was a couple of years back when they lost the Leinster final to Meath when they actually should have won it, but that's water under several bridges now.

I was talking to a fella the other day in Dublin and he told me he was going up to see his father, Frank Higgins, from Tyrone. 'Frank Higgins!' I said. 'Gee, I remember when he played for Tyrone in 1956 and 1957.' I was able to give him the whole Tyrone team who lined out in 1956. He was going home to talk to his dad and tell him, and he said he won't believe it. His father is related in some way to the Hartes, as in Mickey Harte, the number 1 Tyrone manager. So it just goes to show that it does go through the genes.

It's not all about the players. There have been some magnificent managers. Mick O'Dwyer was the manager of Kerry during their golden period, and then he went to Kildare and won a Leinster title with them and brought them to an All-Ireland final. Then he went to Wicklow, and they had the greatest spell in their history.

Mick was a great man-to-man! He wasn't confused by tactics and all sorts of gobbledygook: he just got on with it and trained his teams to the nth degree so they were always fit. If you are fit there are loads of things you can do that you wouldn't even attempt to do if you weren't fit. It's basic logic. Mick made sure his players got even the basics like this right. He took nothing for granted.

He also had the tradition of Kerry, and they were great footballers—I mean great footballers like Ger Power, John Egan, Eoin Liston, Ogie Moran, Pat Spillane, Jack O'Shea, Charlie Nelligan, and John O'Keeffe. To be able to rattle them out of my head shows you how iconic they are, that people like myself can remember them all still.

Kevin Heffernan of Dublin may not have had as good raw material to work with as O'Dwyer and yet he produced wonderful results with them. Dublin won the All-Ireland in 1974; in 1975 they were beaten by Kerry. They won again in 1976; they were in the finals in 1977, 1978, 1979. Tony Hanahoe was captain for these four-in-a-row All-Ireland final teams, winning one. When Keaveney was at his peak that was a great Dublin team for results and bringing the crowd with them. That was a special side to watch. If they had managed to win more than the one All-Ireland you could put up a strong argument for them being one of the greatest sides of all times.

Seán Boylan was another manager who had a great run with Meath. He produced wonderful teams with the likes of Colm O'Rourke, Bernard Flynn, Brian Stafford, David Beggy, Liam Hayes, Gerry

McEntee and Mick Lyons. They had a great spell in the 1980s, into the 1990s.

Of course if you are going to mention great GAA managers then Mickey Harte of Tyrone is up there among the best. Mickey is a smart man, academically smart and worldly-wise, and not a shouter. He may have to shout on the training-ground and in the dressing-room, but he is essentially quiet and gentlemanly. Again like the others, he had great footballers to call on; when you have great players you can trust them for a start.

Joe Kernan of Armagh is another great manager. He brought Armagh to the All-Ireland, which they won in 2002. Jim McGuinness, the Donegal supremo, is a very brainy and very smart man. You would think he is double-thinking you all the time. I remember when they won the All-Ireland in 2012, I observed Donegal through the earlier part of that run and they played a defensive game that people didn't like, but Donegal people loved it; it's hard not to love something when it's working and you're winning games. On one occasion they had no forwards, with the aforementioned Michael Murphy back in his own half! Everyone thought they would be like that for the 2012 championship, and then they were the bloody opposite: from the very start they opened with a brilliant goal and then another one from the other corner from McFadden.

There are great managers and great teams, but I am a player's man first and foremost, and I think the players can make the team. If I had to make a list of all the sportsmen who made my kettle boil, without hesitation Mick O'Connell would be right up there in the list. A Kerry midfielder in the late 1950s and early 1960s, I am sure most would agree that for pure aesthetics he was the most beautiful player. Unfortunately it was an era when there was a lot of rough stuff in Gaelic football, and poorer teams would try and rough him up, and I don't think he was the best man to defend himself. He was gorgeous to watch, though.

If you wanted to pick a top-twenty list you could practically go with the great Kerry players. When you get down to it you could pick all of Kerry, with the likes of Jack O'Shea, Mick O'Connell, Darragh Ó Sé,

Páidí Ó Sé, Pat Spillane, Mikey Sheehy, Colm Cooper, John Egan, John O'Keeffe. You could really pick an all-Kerry side, but you can't do that either.

I have thought a lot about this, and then you have the three or four Dubs who would also be in the running for it. The best Meath footballer of my time for skill and everything would be Trevor Giles, and Colm O'Rourke would have been great also; but Giles would be like Beckenbauer.

Chapter 7 ⌒

MY FAVOURITE GAA FOOTBALLERS

For the greatest players I've decided I'm going to focus on the last forty years only, from the time when Kerry were the kingpins in the 1970s onwards. It means, of course, I am going to miss out on some of the great glamour figures of the game, like Mick O'Connell of Kerry, Packie McGarty of Leitrim, Mickey Kearns of Sligo, and so many wonderful players who our older readers might say should have been in this list. Well, maybe they should be, so that is why to save all arguments I am going for the last forty years; but what a selection of all-time greats I have!

1. JACK O'SHEA (KERRY)

There is an expression in soccer, 'He's a great box-to-box player,' signifying that he can run the pitch from goal to goal. So in Gaelic football I will call it 'square-to-square'; and Jack O'Shea was certainly that sort of player.

Linking play from his defence to his forwards, catching ball, solo-running ball, kicking, and he was always aware. I think he was one of the best long-kickers out of his hand that I have ever seen.

I actually played with him with the Jimmy Magee All-Stars. I saw him numerous times kicking 50, 60, even 70-yard passes out of his hands with almost unnerving accuracy, because that ball has a mind of its own in his capable hands. He scored goals on that great Kerry team. Jack was great, and there may not have been anyone better.

2. PAT SPILLANE (KERRY)

His range of skills was matched by his inexhaustible energy. He loved the game and always wanted to give it his all. He would have been a star at any age, in any of the football codes—soccer, rugby, Gaelic. He was just immense.

Pat was the first Irish Superstar when he won it in 1979, and the prize was a trip to the Bahamas for the World Superstars competition. Superstars was an American invention for television, launched in 1973, which had famous international stars meeting in competition at sports other than their own special field. Ireland got involved in it through RTE, and I was selected as the show's presenter for every season it ran until NBC dropped it in 1994 because of a decline in ratings.

He was just immense and could do anything. He was a great, great footballer. One day during the World Superstars in the Bahamas, Spillane and I watched some of the other athletes who were also competing in the show, killing time by passing around an American ball to each other. Spillane was fascinated by this and knew quite a bit about the American game. Toying with them, he said, 'You know these fellas who come out to take the kicks—how high do they have to kick it, and how long do they have to kick it for it to be a success?'

They explained to him: 'It would have to be hit long, but it would also have to be high enough to stay so that the players could get up around it and not be offside.'

He asked how long it would have to be hit for that to happen. 'If I hit it up to that boundary fence, would that be long?'

'Oh, Paddy, that would be fantastic.'

And then he asked in mock innocence, 'How high would I have to hit it? Would I have to hit it up to that cloud there?'

'Yep.'

So he asked for a ball.

'But there's one difference,' they told him, 'that when the ball is snapped back from the scrimmage there's ten thousand tons of flesh coming on top of you.'

So they all got involved—even the truck-drivers and the television crew—and somebody snapped the ball back to Pat and, as everyone charged towards him, he kicked it high. Now Pat was a fantastic kicker and a high kicker. He kicked that ball right up to Heaven's door and right down to the perimeter fence. They couldn't believe it, and they kept telling others and kept asking him to show others. Sure Pat could do it with his eyes closed. He actually got two offers to go to American football at that time, one for a New Mexico team and the other from a team in Ohio. They were telling everyone about the Irish footballer who could kick the ball so long and so high.

I was walking across the fields in Clones one day and a slightly irate Tyrone supporter came up to me and said, 'Sure what does Pat Spillane know about Gaelic football?'

'I don't know,' I shrugged, and then added, 'All I know is Pat Spillane has eight All-Ireland medals and nine All-Stars. Apart from that I don't know what he knows about it at all.'

'Message taken,' he responded.

3. PETER CANAVAN (TYRONE)

Peter Canavan could always pick the right moment: he could stay with his marker (or rather his marker could stay with him) until the very last second, and then Canavan would break and make himself a small piece of room but enough for a colleague to find him with a pass. It was as though Canavan had seen the rehearsal or read the script, or both, because he knew where to go and most of all when to go and he was always deadly accurate. He was a magnificent scorer.

He was an absolute central figure in Tyrone's coming of age to win the All-Ireland in 2003. It was a marvellous feat of engineering by Mickey Harte and Canavan.

Canavan was injured, and there was a big doubt over whether he could play in the final; that was the big story the whole week before-hand. The fact of the matter was that he did play, but the rest of us didn't know that he was only there in spirit; but it was the spirit that was going to lift the Tyrone team and their fans who had travelled in their thousands, because Canavan meant so much to them.

Apparently Harte, who was a genius of a manager, said to him: 'Go out and play for as long as you can and score as often as you can and then come off, because I know you're not up to it.'

He went out and scored five points in the All-Ireland final and was then replaced. For the last ten or fifteen minutes of the game, when Tyrone needed a lift, what happened? Canavan came back on and the whole place erupted; it was like an explosion. There was an outburst of Tyrone fervour to lift the stadium. To have their biggest star coming back, though injured, and still manage to guide them to an All-Ireland victory was something else to witness. There are no doubts about Canavan being in my top three. He is one of the greatest I have ever seen.

4. MAURICE FITZGERALD (KERRY)

He had two great feet, a sure creative brain and a range of almost unrivalled attacking ideas in football. He was a true genius who ignited every occasion he was involved in. He could kick with either foot; he could score at speed; he could score from laid-back situations and score from distance. He was truly a *different class*.

5. MARTIN McHUGH (DONEGAL)

He is perhaps the best Donegal footballer ever. In 1992 Donegal won the All-Ireland for the first time, and the next time they won it was 2012; his son Mark was on the Donegal team, and is also a very good player.

Martin was a brilliant play-maker. He knew then and still knows now as an analyst so much about the game. He could always find space and was able to exploit it, and he too was truly a *different class*.

6. MATT CONNOR (OFFALY)

Offaly's greatest forward, without a doubt. He was an expert kicker with either foot and remarkably consistent. He knew the game inside out and was a great leader, because he could see the game pass.

I remember he played in a charity soccer match in St Mel's Park in Athlone, as a guest, and the lads from the soccer couldn't believe that this fella coming from Gaelic football could play so well. He was able to spread passes around the field with both feet. He was astonishing.

Sadly, he had a terrible accident. He was a garda, and he was going home at Christmas time and had a serious accident, which didn't leave a mark on him but broke his back, or some sort of damage that paralysed him. He has been in a wheelchair since. He was at the height of his fame at that time, you can take my word on this, and there were very few people as good as or better than Matt Connor from Walsh Island.

7. LARRY TOMPKINS (CORK)
Larry played for Kildare as a sixteen-year-old in the National League and he finished his county career with Cork. He was a super all-rounder: he could fetch; he could carry; and he could kick. Truly a *different class*.

8. TREVOR GILES (MEATH)
Another play-maker, he played centre-half-forward for Meath, but I think if I had the Meath team I would have played him centre-half-back, then the whole game would be in front of him. But it wouldn't matter too much where you played him, because he could see things that nobody else could see; he could spread the ball around him and he was just pure class. Some older Meath readers may disagree, but if you can come up with a better Meath player than Trevor Giles you've got a €45 million player.

9. BRIAN MULLINS (DUBLIN)
A powerhouse at midfield in the great Dublin team of the 1970s, he was a huge man who would have made the second row of international rugby forwards. He was a great catcher of the ball and an immovable object. He was also a great passer of the ball and had huge knowledge of the game. He was a powerpack of a man who could play the physical game but could also play the brain game.

10. ANTHONY TOHILL (DERRY)
A colossal midfielder for Derry, both in height and weight and passing skills. He caught the highest ball with the best and he had definite foot

skills of the very best. He could take free kicks from close in and long distance. He could put the ball on a sixpence, as they used to say. He had a stint in Australian rules, which I don't think he enjoyed too much, but he was big enough and strong enough to play. He was also signed by Manchester United at one time; but his heart was in Gaelic and he came back to that.

11. MIKEY SHEEHY (KERRY)

He once scored two goals and six points in an All-Ireland final, and that was a record. Another record he held with a few others from Kerry is that he has eight All-Ireland medals. He had the eye for the opening and he also had the eye and the impudence to imprint his class on a marginal situation.

He made the marginal situations magical; and anyone who remembers the 1978 All-Ireland final will recall the foul that was given against Paddy Cullen and the ball being handed by Robbie Kelleher to Sheehy to take the 14-yard free. He had the ball on the ground and kicked it off the ground while Cullen, who realised something was afoot, was running back to try and prevent it and couldn't quite make it.

The late Con Houlihan wrote at the time that he was like a housewife being out in the yard and smelling the bread burning and running into the kitchen to try and take it out of the range in time.

For that alone Mikey would have to be among the all-time greats. The boot with which he scored the goal was asked for and given to Paddy Cullen as a gift. They had a friendship between the Kerry and Dublin players, which is one of the great things about Gaelic football.

12. THE Ó SÉ FAMILY (KERRY)

There were three brothers who played on the Kerry team up until recently: Darragh, Tomás and Marc. And sure one is as good as the other. They were nephews of the legendary Páidí, who died recently. Darragh in midfield was a wonderful player; he was a warrior in the true sense and he was also extremely skilful. He caught balls under his own crossbar when Kerry might have been on the defensive, and he was able to press forward attacks when Kerry would be on the offensive. So he was a link man at midfield, and there would be few better than him, even though Kerry have produced some of the greatest midfielders in history. Even in my time it produced Bob Stack, Paddy Kennedy, Mick O'Connell (the most elegant of them all), Jack O'Shea and Darragh Ó Sé. There are so many in these Gaelic teams that you would be all day at naming them, as they all deserve a shout.

13. KEVIN MORAN (DUBLIN)

He came onto the Dublin All-Ireland team of 1976 and was with them for a span of almost four years, during which he was the best centre-half-back that eyes could see. He was wonderful, and he was at Manchester United at the time. He played in the All-Ireland final of 1978, when he pulled a hamstring early in the game, and it is a fact that you just can't play with a pulled hamstring, but he did, because he was just unbeatable, unmovable, strong as a horse. He got a blow on the head that day, so he finished the game limping and with a bandaged head like a turban, and that was the state in which he arrived back to Dave Sexton, the manager of Manchester United, on the Monday! I was going away that Monday after being at the All-Ireland, and Moran was on the same plane. 'Wait until they see me at Manchester; they'll wonder what was I at yesterday! Sure you were there, Jimmy; you saw it; I might have to call you as a witness!' he said jokingly.

Kevin was just sensational. The first man to be sent off in an FA Cup final, by a referee called Willis, for a tackle on Peter Reid, who later played for England in the famous Maradona World Cup match. But his red card in the FA Cup final is no longer an anomaly, as two other players have since been sent off. José Antonio Reyes and Pablo Zabaleta are the other two players who also hold this dubious honour.

I felt sorry for poor old Kevin seeing red in the FA Cup final, because there really wasn't a dirty stroke in him. I know he hit him hard, and sure you have to hit these fellas hard, for there's no use if you don't hit them hard: they will only come back for more. I think for the occasion he should not have been sent off. There have been worse tackles before and since without players even seeing yellow, never mind red.

14. JOHN EGAN (KERRY)

Now he was a powerful Kerry forward whose physique was as formidable as his attacking skills. A Kerry supremo in the greatest era.

15. COLM COOPER (KERRY)

He is class in his every movement; he would conjure up scores outside the range of every normal mortal. He was known as the Gooch, and there was no better: take my word for it that he had few equals.

16. BERNARD BROGAN (DUBLIN)

He has the same first name as his father, who won an All-Ireland in Dublin's golden era. Given a chance at a score he was almost unstoppable; he was nearly always on target when he was within range and able to take scores with both left and right foot. He and his brother Alan were a formidable duo in Dublin teams of later times.

17. GLENN RYAN (KILDARE)

He was one of the best centre-backs of his era, thanks to a driving force, a football brain and a complete knowledge of the number 6 position. He went on later to be a coach for Longford, who he did very well with, and produced some good footballers there. He was maybe Kildare's best player ever, but there were other great players from the county, like Pat Mangan, Kevin Kelly and Jack Donnelly. But I doubt if there was ever better than Glenn Ryan, and certainly not one better at centre-half-back.

18. TOMÁS AND PÁIDÍ Ó SÉ (KERRY)

All the things I said about Darragh Ó Sé you can say about Tomás, who played in the same position as his famous uncle, Páidí, at right-half-back, or he could play anywhere. He was that sort of footballer, the same as Páidí. He had the same strength, almost replicating that of his famous uncle.

19. MICHAEL MURPHY (DONEGAL)

He is still only in his early twenties, and if he never kicks another ball he will always be remembered for the first goal he scored for Donegal in the 2012 All-Ireland final. Receiving a great foot pass from Karl Lacy, Murphy went for it. It was a magnificent sight watching him as he turned the defender, landed on the ground, and as he landed hit the shot with his right foot. Well, if you had ten Gordon Bankses in goal they wouldn't have stopped it from rippling the net. On that alone his reputation will live for ever, but of course he is much more than that. He was captain of Donegal that day. Amazingly, he was captain when he was a teenager. He is a great footballer, and he is going to be even better.

20. SEÁN CAVANAGH (TYRONE)

He has been around for years and he is still really only a young player! He plays with a class pace and power. He is able to catch the ball and fight for the ball with the best of them. He would be the nearest to Jack O'Shea I have seen. He really would take some beating in any company, in any class, by anyone down through the years.

21. GREG BLANEY (DOWN)

A brilliant forward who you could rely on to score when it counts. The best way for me to describe him is like this: he always played in the style of a man who seemed to know what the game was going to be like and had seen the rehearsals beforehand and was able to follow the instructions of the director.

22. SÉAMUS MOYNIHAN (KERRY)

Here was a man who could play anywhere, and probably did. I think that maybe he sacrificed his very best years to become Kerry's full-back, because had he not done that he would have been centre-half-back, midfield, wing half—anywhere you like. He was just one of those very, very special players and among the greatest Kerry footballers who ever lived, which in itself is saying something, because Kerry is not the kingdom of football for nothing.

23. DERMOT EARLEY AND DERMOT EARLEY (ROSCOMMON)

One a father, one a son. Dermot senior could high-catch, kick long, solo run, plant free kicks. He was a great leader of men, on and off the field, and probably Roscommon's best ever, in the esteemed company of Gerry O'Malley.

24. EAMONN O'HARA (SLIGO)

He once scored a great goal in the not-too-distant past in the Connacht championship, where he soloed with one foot and hit the shot with the other, which, if nothing else, makes him worthy of inclusion. But there is a lot more to O'Hara who has played for nearly twenty years with his native Sligo without any great rewards. But not all the great footballers, sadly, got to play for the big teams.

25. KIERAN McGEENEY (ARMAGH)

He was the main play-maker, captain and centre-half-back in that wonderful Armagh team that won the All-Ireland, and then he went on as coach for Kildare.

26. JIMMY KEAVENEY (DUBLIN)

He was one of the best footballers there ever was. He was really retired from the game in 1974 when Dublin played Wexford in the first round of the championship, and they didn't play too well. The late Kevin Heffernan was Dublin manager, and he got on to Keaveney that evening and asked him if he was at the game that day, and didn't they do great. Heffernan said to him, 'If one man came back to us we would have a real chance at the All-Ireland.' And he asked him would he come back, and then said, 'See you at training on Tuesday.' Keaveney had so much respect for Heffernan that he turned up, and the following Sunday he played for Dublin against Louth and scored eight points. In September that year Dublin were All-Ireland champions, and Keaveney was one of the stars.

Ten years later Dublin's marquee forward was the brilliant Barney Rock, from a legendary GAA family.

———

There, by the grace of God, and everybody else who counts, are twenty-six plus of the best Gaelic footballers who have ever put on knicks and a jersey. I could probably name another twenty-five even off the top of my head, but I couldn't name another twenty-five who are better. I could have included others, such as, say, Jason Sherlock, because I loved him as a player and could have selected him, and I probably should have put him in; but there's the list.

Chapter 8 ～

I MY FAVOURITE HURLERS

You have thirty hurlers who fit the bill, I think. 'What bill?' I hear you ask. I mean a *different class*. I am starting at a certain time, around the same period as the footballers, going back only forty years, which means I am leaving out brilliant players like Christy Ring, Mick Mackey, and John Keane of Waterford.

1. D. J. CAREY (KILKENNY)

A genius with the ball. He is a magician at funnelling out opportunities. We are talking about a master hurler and a truly great player. I don't think I have ever seen better than D. J. Carey.

2. MARTIN QUIGLEY (WEXFORD)

Four Quigley brothers played in the All-Ireland final of 1970: Martin, Dan, John and Pat. I don't think the rest of them would mind too much if I say that Martin was one of the very, very best for Wexford. He could play anywhere, but he usually played in any of the forward positions.

3. HENRY SHEFFLIN (KILKENNY)

He is the leading championship scorer of all time, which means his total has surpassed those of Christy Ring, Mick Mackey, Jimmy Langton, even his own county man Eddie Keher. When I was ill in hospital D. J. Carey came in to see me. I recounted a story to him about what Eddie Keher said about him. I did a quiz one night back in the late '80s in Kilkenny with Eddie, who won six All-Irelands and was one of the most prolific scorers of all time. We were talking about the greatest players of all time, and he said, 'You love names, Jimmy. There's a young boy in Kilkenny, and if he keeps at it and doesn't get ill and stays in love with the game he is going to be the greatest of them all. And his name is D. J. Carey. You should remember that name.'

DJ couldn't believe that Eddie Keher had spoken so highly of him. He thought that was some tribute. 'I'm going to give you one now, Jimmy. There's another young fella coming along who will be better than any of us. So remember the name: the name is Henry Shefflin.'

Ten years ago I went into the Kilkenny dressing-room after they had just won the League, and I went over and sat beside Shefflin and told him, 'I'm going to tell you a story about D. J. Carey and Eddie Keher.' As I began to tell him, I glanced over to the other corner and saw that D. J. Carey and Henry Shefflin were actually in the room.

After I'd finished, Shefflin said, 'Did D. J. Carey say that about me?' 'He certainly did.'

DJ was right too about Shefflin, who has just become the first player ever to win ten All-Stars, as well as nine All-Ireland medals, which is going to be an almost impossible feat for anybody to repeat.

4. JIMMY BARRY MURPHY (CORK)

One of Cork's heroic Gaelic players in both hurling and football. There are very few who are better than Jimmy Barry Murphy. He is a great figure, and he had two spells as manager in Cork hurling and has been chief coach.

5. EOIN KELLY (TIPPERARY)

He was in the Tipperary senior team as a minor and played until well into his thirties. He was a fantastic player, with great speed off the mark and a wonderful shot. He was an amazingly accurate player.

6. JAMES O'CONNOR (CLARE)

Everyone in hurling knew him as Jamesy. I once saw his little pile of hurleys, and on them he had imprinted his name as James O'Connor, so because of that I call him James. I suppose he has the wrists of a Kilkenny man, although as far as I know he has no Kilkenny con-nections, but that wrist work makes him a very special kind of player.

He was on the teams that won the All-Ireland in 1995 and again in 1997.

7. NICHOLAS ENGLISH (TIPPERARY)

In 1989 he scored what I would call a fantastic goal for Tipp against Antrim in the All-Ireland final. It was a fabulous full volley from across the right wing—a goal with force. It was the goal that brought the championship to Tipperary. It wasn't just that goal, though: there were loads of other things about him that would make him worthy of being described as a *different class*. He once scored a great goal in a Munster championship game with his foot; now you may say that's not a big deal, but it was a brilliant goal, because he was left in a tight angled position where if he didn't kick it he would miss the shot at goal. So he kicked it and he bent it. He proved that day that it's possible to bend a sliotar with your foot.

8. JOE COONEY (GALWAY)

He came from a family of great hurlers, but with all due respect to his siblings, Joe is probably the best of the lot.

9. JOHNNY LEAHY (TIPPERARY)

He comes from Mullinahone, which is perhaps more a football area, but Leahy was different. His blend of power, innate hurling skills and physical presence meant he could match anyone from any county.

10. CIARÁN CAREY (LIMERICK)

You could play this fella practically anywhere, either at half-back or midfield or even at half-forward if you wanted to. He had few betters and seldom had he any peers. He had a long stride, and when he went on a run he was unstoppable really. He also had a great long puck. He could puck with accurate passes, and he could do short ones as well. He scored a couple of great points.

11. SEÁN McMAHON (CLARE)

He was a centre-half-back of great presence. He linked wing-backs with almost seamless strokes of hurling.

12. JOE CANNING (GALWAY)

A born star. As a minor Joe showed the skills, greatness and hurling nous of men twice his age. He brought his class through groundwork to senior level, and he has seen an avalanche of scores since he became a senior figure. He is a wonderful player who can come outfield, grab a ball, make little passes. There is one great no-show pass that is on the all-time list of highlights that you see on hurling shows at the end of the year.

13. GER HENDERSON (KILKENNY)

He was a brilliant centre-half-back. He was one of three brothers who played for the county. John played corner-back and his brother Pat played centre-half-back before Ger.

14. TONY BROWN (WATERFORD)

One of Waterford's greatest players ever. He was happy and comfortable on the ball in any position in the midfield area, from half-back to half-forward and especially around conventional midfield.

15. JOHNNY MULLANE (WATERFORD)

He only retired in 2013, but he was as sharp as steel, an edgy player, right up until his retirement. You always saw him at the top of his game, and he was not to be taken lightly by the opposition. He took no prisoners and didn't expect any favours. He was really, really good.

16. FRANK CUMMINS (KILKENNY)

He was one of the game's all-time greats. A powerful, bulky man, but he had the quickness of movement and thought that make him a star.

17. KEN McGRATH (WATERFORD)

A centre-half-back who could play in any position really: centre-half-forward, midfield; he could even play full-back. Give him a hurley and he could play anywhere. That's the type of player a team always needs.

18. TONY DORAN (WEXFORD)

Tony is from Buffers Alley, the local club in the villages of Kilmuckridge and Monamolin. Tony was adept at catching the ball and ripping his way through full-back lines and bursting the net. He was on the 1968 team and was a wonderful Wexford hurler.

19. PAUL FLYNN (WATERFORD)

He was one of the best and greatest forwards we have ever seen. He is now out of the senior inter-county game but is a really terrific player. In the early stages of his career he was going to be a footballer; in fact he had trials in England in soccer.

20. J. J. DELANEY (KILKENNY)

He was a full-back and one of the very best at wing-back.

21. JOHN CONNOLLY (GALWAY)

An original All-Star and a leader of teams. A leader of Galway and a leader of the family in Castlegar. His brothers Michael and Joe were also in the Galway inter-county hurlers squad.

22. TONY KEILY (GALWAY)

You can't go past Galway without mentioning Tony, the king of centre-half-backs for that county.

23. PAT FOX (TIPPERARY)

He began life as a defender and carried on right through, despite having a bad leg that had been operated on and was only held together—the joke was 'held together by thread,' but whatever it was held together with it was gold as far as Tipp was concerned, because he was truly a forward of a *different class*.

24. MARTIN STOREY (WEXFORD)

A star in Wexford's mighty All-Ireland of 1996. Martin was the leader of the attack, score-maker, score-taker.

25. PAT HARTIGAN (LIMERICK)

He was the prince of full-backs who were in the first five All-Stars. Unfortunately an eye injury after getting hit with a ball put an end to his career.

26. GEORGE O'CONNOR (WEXFORD)

He played both hurling and football for Wexford and for Leinster. A great player with skill. He was a hard player, but you can't really be soft and play top-class hurling.

27. SEÁN ÓG Ó hAILPÍN (CORK)

He's probably the best-known GAA player with a Fijian mother and Co. Fermanagh father. He is one of Cork's legendary hurlers and foot-ballers who has won numerous awards, including three All-Ireland medals. He also won three consecutive All-Star awards. He is still on the cusp of the game.

28. BRIAN WHELEHAN (OFFALY)

He was on the Team of the Millennium, which says enough. He was right half-back, but he has played in other positions for Offaly. A general all-rounder, with great control of the stick and a great man-marker, who ran his socks off and could brilliantly read the game and see positions. No wonder he was on the Team of the Millennium, as he really was a class apart.

29. TOMMY WALSH (KILKENNY)

He is the best right-half-back in the world, but he's a play-anywhere man. He has all sorts of proficiencies in the forward line and the backs, but I think latterly he has been number 5, and in this position he is unbeatable.

30. ÉAMONN CREGAN (LIMERICK)

He is my final name in this long list of exceptional hurlers. A fantastic forward; and yet, despite the fact that he was a free-scoring corner-forward and one of the best that ever put on the green jersey of Limerick, and of course an All-Star as well, it's ironic that the match that he should be best remembered for is the All-Ireland final of 1973, when he was moved by Limerick from his forward position to centre-half-back, especially to mark the Kilkenny danger man Pat Delaney. How well did he mark him? Well, the answer is in the final score line: the All-Ireland was won by Limerick for the first time since 1940, and they haven't won it since! There is a particular sadness for players who come from weak counties that are never going to win anything.

Chapter 9 ～

| THE BOYS IN GREEN

B efore Jack Charlton made world soccer sit up and take notice of Ireland, we had top-quality players under Johnny Giles—and perhaps they underachieved; but Eoin Hand was possibly the unluckiest Irish manager. He nearly got us to the finals in Spain. We were only beaten for a place in it by France on goal difference. Of course it was almost a case of history repeating itself under Trapattoni when Ireland were unceremoniously robbed of the chance of playing in the World Cup by that infamous hand ball by Thierry Henry.

The difference is that while Henry's French team imploded at the 2010 World Cup, Ireland under Eoin Hand had only lost out on goal difference to a French side that went on to be become European champions. They had all the great stars, like Giresse and Platini—all those sort of fellas—and yet Ireland were right up there with them to the end. The two teams in our group were France, who got to the semi-final, and Belgium, who got the quarter-final.

If we had qualified, Eoin would have been able to write his own contract after that, and yet he was done out of it. He was the unluckiest man in Irish soccer, without any doubt.

As a manager, Eoin was a mix of the Giles and the Charlton. He was a centre-half himself, so he has a natural defensive outlook, yet he didn't play boring defensive football but rather had an awareness of what was needed at the back. If you look at Hand's teams, he had a lot of goals and he gave a free hand to a lot of his really good forwards, like Frank Stapleton, Don Givens and Ray Treacy.

Speaking of Don Givens, any time his name is mentioned it conjures up images for me of what is possibly the greatest day in Irish soccer, in September 1974, when Ireland took on the USSR. I remember it for three things—in ascending order: firstly, a fella called Terry Mancini was playing for Ireland at centre-back, and on a corner kick he got into a bit of a mess with the Soviet player, and the two of them were sent off. So we had Mancini making his first appearance in Dublin, and Ireland were down to ten players.

The second thing I remember it for was the fact that it was also Liam Brady's debut for Ireland. Giles had picked him after he played a game against Arsenal and saw up close how talented Brady was. I was actually at that game.

And the third reason I recall this fantastic game is the hat trick by Don Givens, who later on got four goals against Turkey and thus became the first Irishman ever to score four goals in a European Championship game. Paddy Moore had scored four goals before, in 1934 in a World Cup qualifier at Dalymount Park—making him the first player in the world to score four goals in a World Cup match.

It was a stellar performance by Ireland against the Soviet Union. The stadium was more than packed that day. Giles had a great team. The Soviets must have been shocked, as they would have been favourites, but Giles was very astute and he had put together a very good team. Ray Treacy was largely responsible for Givens's goals by helping bustle guys out of it or making the final pass. Joe Kinnear was also in that team, who went on to become the manager of Wimbledon; and then there was Giles himself, who for my money was probably Ireland's best player ever.

Givens had to have a bit of luck that day, but he also had a lot of style and skill. Givens is one of the best strikers we ever had. He had a good pace and physical strength, which, allied to pace, are two great assets for a footballer. Also, he had the ability to put the ball away. He comes from a sporting family: his brother John played in the League of Ireland, and his father played hurling for Limerick and played in an All-Ireland final. John played for many of the clubs around the Dublin area and for Athlone Town FC. He never got to the premiership even though he was a very good player. Don had a great pace and he had a great period with Queen's Park Rangers when they had a good team, with Gerry Francis and Stan Bowles.

By the way, Givens followed that game against the USSR by scoring in the 1-1 draw with Turkey and then getting all four goals in the 4-0 victory over Turkey in the final game of the group.

We have had many good players over the years, like all the aforementioned, but never had enough in depth to be a really, really good team, for which you need to have more than thirteen players. Charlton probably had the best players available: he had the likes of Mark Lawrenson, Mick McCarthy, Kevin Moran, the peerless Paul McGrath, Dave O'Leary, Jim Holmes, Dave Langan, Frank Stapleton, Tony Grealish, Gerry Daly and Ronnie Whelan.

A lot of Irish people will remember that he had (think about these for centre-halfs) Paul McGrath at right-back and Ronnie Whelan at left-back, and he had Mark Lawrenson in midfield, and at centre-half he had Moran and McCarthy. It was an embarrassment of riches.

You can't dispute Charlton's record and would have to declare him indisputably the best manager Ireland has had in living memory, in terms of results.

The exhibition matches you kind of put to one side and say, 'Ah, they don't matter.' But everybody could sense that Ireland were growing into a formidable side after the famous friendly against Brazil in 1987, making Ireland the first Celtic country to beat the South Americans.

Brazil, of course, are the top name in football for national teams. They have always produced stars. On that occasion the stand-out for me was we had Liam Brady, who was Brazilian in his ability. You could look at him and say you could put a yellow shirt on him and blue shorts and he could be a Brazilian—he was of that standard. He picked his spot and scored a goal that would have made even Pelé proud. Wonderful! I remember thinking after that game, Charlton is really making inroads with this squad. Maybe we can finally qualify for a major tournament.

Sadly, it didn't end well for Brady under Charlton. He was taken off in a friendly against Germany before half time. In his autobiography Charlton claimed he did so because Brady wasn't playing the high-tempo, pressing game he demanded and he feared we could lose the match. That's his argument anyway. Brady was also taken off in his testimonial against Finland. People were aghast. It's hard to defend a manager taking off a player in his own testimonial, isn't it?

Later on there was a big dinner for Liam and everybody who was anybody was there; it was very nicely done, and naturally Charlton was there. I was one of the ones who spoke at it. Jack was asked to go up onto the stage to say a few words too. But, Jack being Jack, he stood up and said: 'People often say to me that by taking off Liam did I make a mistake.' Now all Liam's family were at this dinner, his father and mother, brothers, aunts and uncles. 'I did make a mistake: I should have brought him off sooner.'

The reaction was pretty sharp, but Jack motored on regardless. Jack was Jack, as I say. I thought it was rude, because if you were in an Irish situation you don't insult the father and mother anyway, whatever about insulting the lad himself.

Sadly, Brady didn't get to play at Euro '88 or Italia '90.

Charlton was lucky to get the Irish job; there were a load of lads lined up to take it. The votes didn't add up. It's a fact that Charlton was an also-ran after the first vote, and when they voted again there was a sort of tie-break and he was the winner. So two or three had to have changed their minds.

I don't think anyone would have done it any better. Jack took the task in hand. Jack wasn't into science in any fashion: he was a straight-forward man, get up and get at them was his attitude. His great phrase was 'Put 'em under pressure,' and it had a certain merit. It was very uncouth, to be honest, but it worked.

If you look at it on paper and what they were capable of it probably was technically the best Irish team, but he didn't allow them to show that they were technically good. Maybe that's why he didn't like Brady. He even sidelined David O'Leary because he wouldn't go to Iceland, as he had already arranged his holidays, which was a perfectly okay thing to do; but Jack couldn't see that: he thought you had to live and die football. Ironically, David was the man who then took the penalty that mattered against Romania.

Jack wanted them to 'put 'em under pressure,' and he had John Aldridge—who was a great striker for lots of clubs, mostly Liverpool—and he didn't score at all for Ireland. His job was not to allow them to play the ball down the back, to basically be the first defender. It may have looked like a willy-nilly system, but it worked, up to a point.

Jack's plan was about containing the other team for long enough and praying that maybe you could snatch a goal yourself. It was nearly a perfect thing, but once you went behind it was very difficult, because you didn't have the football set-up to attack.

He got us to the European Championship and two World Cups, a record that nobody since has ever matched. The way things are going at the moment I doubt we'll see anybody equal his record in the foreseeable future.

Yet despite all his success, there are very few memorable games, funny enough, under Charlton. Ireland beating England was always a great thrill—no matter what sort of rubbish the game was. We were actually the first team to beat England on their home soil, all the way back in 1949 at Goodison Park in Liverpool. I remember that game. I can recall Henry Rose, who was a writer in the *Daily Express*, and he was doing a preview of the match and saying that Ireland had no chance (which, in fairness to him, they hadn't). One of the things he said was, 'I will eat my hat if England don't win this game.' And he was made to eat his hat the next day!

But Stuttgart '88 against England will probably stand out as our best result ever, alongside beating Italy at USA '94. Funny enough, Ray Houghton scored both goals in those two games, two of the most important goals that Ireland has ever scored in competition, with a header and a left foot—and he is a right-footed player.

England was all over us, but that's no good unless they put the ball in on the night. Whatever Charlton did, it worked! Gary Lineker did everything but score a hat trick that day.

Ireland dominated the USSR in the next match, and we got a fantastic goal with Ronnie Whelan when he hit it with his shin, but he hit it perfectly. It was a perfect trajectory; it was a great goal, and who would have known that it was with his shin, except he admitted it himself! It was as if we were playing total football, Dutch-style, in that game against the ussr. Somebody probably said during that game, 'Feck this, we'll pass the ball!' And so they did, and they played football. Sure Jack wouldn't give out to you for that! If it was going well he would say, 'So what?' and shrug.

But Jack went ballistic when it didn't work out against Italy at Italia '90, when a Kevin Sheedy pass to John Aldridge was intercepted and the Italians then scored.

Charlton once told me about that game. 'I said to the fellas, "I want you to play it over the top." And Kevin Sheedy says, "We don't do that at Everton; we play to feet." I told him, "I don't care what you do at Everton, this is not Everton, and don't give us that insubordination, play it over the top." Sheedy says, "But—" I said, "No buts at all, play it over the top. Get it?" Sheedy then says, "Do you mean if I have the ball I don't pass it to one of my own team?" "Correct."

'So what happens in the game? Sheedy has the ball. Aldridge is there and calls for it. Sheedy passes it to Aldridge and it bounces away from him. The Italians get it, run it down, cross, and it comes to your man Donadoni, and he has a shot. I ask Packie for one save; he can only parry it away, and that fella Schillaci got the only goal. It was hard luck for Packie, bad control by Aldridge, but it wasn't their fault: it was Sheedy who didn't do as he was told. Had he done what he was told they wouldn't have got the ball and they wouldn't have got that goal.'

'Jeepers, Jack, that simplifies it,' I replied.

We were unlucky in our last game in Euro '88 not to get out of the group when we lost by a fluky goal to the Netherlands, who eventually beat the ussr in the final. But, in fairness, the Dutch then dominated us in that game. The Dutch goal was dodgy offside. The Netherlands are just a wonderful team—look at the players they had: Marco van Basten, Ruud Gullit and Frank Rijkaard, Ronald Koeman . . .

To be blunt, our group games in Italia '90 were unmemorable at best; and the second-round game against Romania was a strange match. It's incredible the way life turns. It was very warm weather. You had the whole David O'Leary thing; he was basically the 'spy who came in from the cold' that day. Jack wouldn't have been in love with him, as far as I know. As it turned out, Steve Staunton was feeling the heat badly during the closing stages of the game, and Charlton made a change and he brought on Dave O'Leary in the dying minute, and it then went to penalties. Of all the men, Dave said he would take the last one. Charlton was standing on the side-line, and he had no say in the matter. Everybody was saying, 'Is he really going to take the penalty?' George Hamilton said, 'A nation holds its breath.' And fair play to David, he bloody stuffed it away! That was after Packie had saved a penalty from Daniel Timofte. The Romanian is infamous back in Packie Bonner's home place of Burtonport, Co. Donegal, where some of the local boys named their fishing boat *Timofte*.

It was fantastic when Charlton managed to get us out of a fairly tight group to qualify for USA '94. It was extra-special to be working at the World Cup there, because I was born in New York. We had a great match in the Giants Stadium, and I don't think anybody will ever forget Ray Houghton's beautiful slot chip over the Italian goalkeeper Pagliuca's head that ended up in the net. He will also obviously be fondly remembered for his header against England in Euro '88. But it was fantastic to get one over on the Italians after they beat us in the quarter-final of the previous World Cup by the same score line of 1-0. Italy, of course, got all the way to the final in '94—only losing to Brazil on penalties, meaning that Ireland were the only team to actually beat them during ninety minutes in that particular World Cup.

It was a very tight group, with all four teams (Mexico, Italy, Norway and ourselves) ending up on four points. It was John Aldridge's goal against Mexico that got us ahead of Italy and Norway and out of the group.

But some of our performances were absolutely terrible. But yet again the argument put forward was, 'The end justifies the means.' Alas, no. For me the end does not justify the means. If I was the coach, yes, the end would justify the means, but if I am a paying spectator it doesn't. I know that is something of a contradiction, but it is the truth. Who in their right mind wants to be bored to death by an unexciting game?

Anyway, there was no justifying our performance against the Dutch. Yes, there's the excuse of the hot weather—but the Dutch had to deal with the same conditions too. FIFA should have demanded that games like this be played in the evening, but they were obviously more concerned about scheduling the games to please the television stations. There was no way we were going to be able to play our pressing game against the Dutch, as we had against the Italians in New Jersey. It says a lot about the quality of our players back then that they were officially the only team to beat the Italians in that tournament: the Brazilians only won the final itself by beating the Italians on penalties.

As soon as the Dutch match kicked off, all I was thinking was, 'Here we go again!' It was a terrible mistake for the first goal with a stupid back pass, and Bonner should have saved the second. Nothing went our way that day; even Paul McGrath had a goal disallowed.

It all came to a crashing halt in 1995 for Charlton. We should have qualified for Euro '96, but we were forced into a play-off against the Dutch. We should have had a chance, considering the game was being played in Anfield, but we were bloody hammered. There was no doubt about that. They were just better than us. The wagon imploded. I think Jack had given up by then, and he said goodbye publicly that night. He had a great run. Irish people were good to him and loved him, and he loved them also.

Next up was Mick McCarthy, who had quite a good spell by qualifying for a World Cup too. But Saipan was the beginning of the end for him. Saipan was the watershed for him and Roy Keane, who could have been in any of the aforementioned teams: he could have gone into Giles's team, Charlton's team—anyone's. We had Duff and Robbie Keane, we also had Shay Given in goal, and we had Richard Dunne coming along. John O'Shea was making shapes; we had enough fairly decent players . . . but without Roy Keane we weren't ever going to be at the races. I blame both Roy and Mick for the fall-out. I don't think Mick should have confronted him in the way he did in front of all the players, and I don't think Roy should have used such language and then stormed off home. Can you imagine what we would have achieved if Keane had played in that World Cup?

We still played some great football. My abiding memory is the German match. Now, that was a hell of a game. We were unlucky to go a goal down, and the whole comeback was brilliant. Robbie Keane scored a fantastic goal in the dying minutes. It was the first time Germany fell apart in any competition—and they just don't fall apart.

You have to wonder if Ireland would have done better if Roy Keane was there. It's hard to say when it's past, but at that time Keane was a really great player and a powerful influence. His work rate alone was worth another half a man anyway. So if you had him in your team he would keep going, and he proved that with Ireland.

Keane was the man who got us to the World Cup. He dragged the team there with his one-man show performances. A good example is the match in Dublin against the Netherlands, when Jason McAteer finally got the goal that knocked the Dutch out and sent us to the World Cup. It was a great game and a brilliant result, considering we played most of it with only ten men. Keane set the pace for that game. He lifted us for those vital games. He would hate anyone dragging their feet after him, and he wouldn't ask anyone to do anything that he wouldn't do himself. His attitude was 'If I can't do it, I won't ask you to do it.'

It was inevitable that McCarthy would go after the Keane fall-out. Next up was Brian Kerr, who had a nice run also, but the powers that be in the media turned against him. I'm not fully sure what happened, but maybe he didn't give them the co-operation they felt they should have had.

Then there was Steve Staunton. He arrived on the scene then with Bobby Robson in tow, and sure they weren't given a fair chance either: people just didn't get a chance. Lance Armstrong got more of a chance than anyone got.

You could have said that Trapattoni was beginning to do just as well as Charlton had until there was an implosion in Poland in 2012, when it just went from bad to worse. It was like an internal illness. We were certainly up against the best teams: we had Spain, who of course won it and are the world champions also, so you can't argue about losing to them. They even hammered Italy in the final. Then we had to face Italy, who were the immediate champions before them and traditionally one of the great teams. And then in our group there was one of the rising countries of Europe, Croatia.

However, the Irish performances were abysmal. I don't like saying it, as there are too many people looking at the game and wanting to point the finger of blame, and looking at the managers, but maybe Trapattoni has to take some of the blame for not making changes.

I, for one, couldn't understand the game against Spain, and I was at it. The game was crying out for a change of plan, and he simply didn't do it. He wasn't giving players likes Wes Hoolahan a game, a brilliant player who was running the show at the time for Norwich. The young fella James McClean didn't get a run either, and he was playing brilliant stuff in the Premiership at the time; as too was his fellow-Derryman Darron Gibson, who also didn't get a run. He famously gave Paul Green a run when Green didn't have a club!

It might be a slight thing of communication breakdown; it might be that he didn't read the papers here; he didn't listen to the radio; and most of all he didn't go to the matches.

Yes, I think it was great that Denis O'Brien was paying his wages, so we could have a top manager—but you expect such a top manager to earn his wages, not just sit by and watch Ireland get ripped apart, game after game. It was as if he didn't learn any lessons from Poland, because we then got hammered by Germany at home, a highly embarrassing 6-1 thrashing.

It's obvious that he should be sacked or fall on his own sword, but to get rid of anybody you have to have somebody better in their place, and I can't see who they could get to replace him. Even now I can't see who they would have as a manager. If I was going for a manager at the time of writing I would opt for Martin O'Neill, who also happens to be from Derry. He is very much one of us, and he would be terrific. He did a fantastic job at Celtic and Leicester. I doubt the FAI have ever been in touch with Martin O'Neill, but I would say he would love to do it.

I don't know if he would accept the job or not, but I think Roy Keane would make a good shape of it, and he wouldn't suffer fools too easily. Roy had bad runs with bad teams, but I think Roy would relish taking over Ireland.

I think Trapattoni will step down at the end of this World Cup qualification if we don't qualify. Germany will win our group, and then after that who knows? It has been part of our life; we have always been like that, part of the dream factory. That's the way it was until Charlton arrived, and we are still at it.

I think Irish people's expectations for the national team are probably too high, and then we are looking for excuses. But still we shouldn't be getting thrashed, like the way we used to put lesser sides like Malta to the sword.

Apart from everything else we are unlucky with a lot of things; for instance the Thierry Henry goal was bad luck. But that's life for you: life is full of downs like that. We don't need much to lift our spirits as a nation: look at Katie Taylor winning in London. The whole country was on a new high after she became the first Irish female boxer to win an Olympic gold medal. Hopefully it won't be too long before a new manager takes over the Irish team and injects the optimism and self-belief that we've been lacking during the past few years. It's hard to imagine us returning to the days of being a *different class* under Jack Charlton (remember under him we were once at number 8 in the FIFA world rankings); but it would be fantastic to see the fighting Irish putting it up to top teams again.

| MAJOR ACHIEVEMENTS

I rish golfers have enjoyed much success down through the decades. For me the two big success stories were Christy O'Connor Senior and young Rory McIlroy, who seems to be jumping back and forward between the number 2 and number 1 spot in the world rankings at the moment. The third-biggest moment is Christy O'Connor Junior in the famous Ryder Cup victory. Amazingly, we won eight majors in three to four years: Harrington with three majors, Clarke with one, McDowell with one, McIlroy with two (US Open and US PGA). Before that, Fred Daly on one.

Without further ado, here is my list of all-time great Irish golfers. In very recent years Irish golf has been on a super high—thanks to the exploits of Pádraig Harrington, Graeme McDowell, Rory McIlroy and Darren Clarke. But before these recent victories the only Irishman to win a major was Fred Daly in the 1940s, when he won the British Open in 1947.

But the best Irish golfer of all time, in my opinion, was Christy O'Connor Senior. He was the best striker of a ball. He would regularly play a driver off the fairway, and very few people could do that back then; even now that is rare. He played in every Ryder Cup during his heyday, and his record was 10 until Nick Faldo beat it. Christy was fantastic.

There wasn't that big a gap between Senior and Junior. Christy's nephew, Christy O'Connor Junior, also played in the Ryder Cup. He was also the bee's knees. He played that famous two-iron shot in the Ryder Cup that sealed victory.

O'Connor Senior could play every club splendidly. If O'Connor was playing now he would be a major star. I wouldn't say he took the greatest care of himself, like being out doing ten-mile runs every morning and doing weights, like you see the fellas doing now.

His nephew has a very funny story about his uncle playing one time against the Spanish champion Seve Ballesteros. 'He was playing with Christy Senior in Portmarnock one day and he came in and rang his father from the telephone in the locker room, and he said (in Spanish), "Father, I play with an old man today—he is almost as good as me!" Brilliant!' Christy recalls, laughing.

In second place, without any hesitation, I'd have Pádraig Harrington. Why Pádraig? I hear you ask. Well, he is simply the best tournament player we ever had, as he won three major ones.

By the time this book comes out McIlroy will probably be the best! Harrington is a great and wonderful competitor. Not many people know this, but he was going to be a footballer before the golf bug got him. His father, who was a close friend of mine, was an All-Ireland footballer from west Cork. Sadly, he died in 2005.

But the GAA's loss was the golfing world's gain. The affable Dubliner made history when he won the 2007 British Open Championship at Carnoustie. The finale was extraordinary, with both Harrington and his main rival, Sergio García, making errors over the final few holes, leading to a head-to-head shoot-out. It went down to the wire: after the emotional roller-coaster of that closing round, in which Harrington made up six strokes on his rival with a 67, Pádraig defeated the Spaniard by a single stroke in a four-hole play-off. In doing so he became the first European to win a major since 1999, and also the first Irishman to triumph at the Open in over sixty years.

At the moment Rory McIlroy is only third on my list. I'm sure he'll move up in my estimation in the not-too-distant future. I remember years ago talking about Rory with people at these dinners that you have to go to. They'd be eagerly telling me, 'Wait until you see Rory; he's fantastic.' So I knew Rory before I ever saw him play. Ah, he's a fantastic golfer, and when he settles down with his new Nike clubs he will clean up. I think he will be right up there with Woods in the history books.

Leabharlanna Poibli Chathair Bhaile Átha Cliath
Dublin City Public Libraries

Next on my list, at number 4, would be Shane Lowry, because he was only the third amateur to win on the European Tour when he won the Irish Open. Back in the good old days there was a great amateur set-up in Ireland, with many great golfers. At that time I was an avid player myself, so I would see these fellas regularly on the golf course.

Darren Clarke would have to be in my top five. He has spent more time on the course than anyone else, I guess—sure he's still on the course! He has two world championship events and a total of twenty-two major tournaments, including three PGA Tours, a staggering fourteen European Tours and three Japan Golf Tours.

Christy O'Connor Junior squeezes into my top six Irish golfers of all time. He has won several Opens and even made that memorable putt to help Europe retain the Ryder Cup in 1989. He remembers being over-shadowed by the legacy of his uncle when he started out as a professional golfer. 'I did at the beginning—very much so. It took about five years. He was really in his prime when I came on the scene and was playing very well. I'd hit a golf shot, and whoever you were playing with might say to you, "That's a great shot, but your uncle would've got it past the bend." He had such an Irish following—he really was the only one . . .' Christy recalls.

I remember there was a fabulous finish by Christy at the Royal Dublin to win the Carroll's Open. The last three holes were a short par 4, a stinking par 4 and a par 5, and he went birdie, birdie and eagle to finish it. Never were the likes of it heard of before or since. He was just a wonderful player. He could make the ball talk, and I bet if you asked Harrington or any of them now they would tell you the same.

O'Connor almost won once; he led the British Open and he held the course record on a couple of occasions, but he had a rough time and blew it. It was a case of so close but yet so far, and he blames himself for failing to win. As he explains it, 'I played the best golf of the four days—even though I shot 64, a new course record in the first round, and that was after thirty-nine years. Of course the record was 65 after thirty-nine years. I beat it. I think I missed only one green, which was quite un-believable in regulation. I took 37 putts, which is like 7 putts too many.

The average putting would be 30 per round. I had 37 that day, which is pretty awful, and that's what lost me the Open.'

Even though it's a team event, we can put Christy's performance in the Ryder Cup back in 1989 right up there as one of the stand-out moments of his career, because he retained the cup for Europe with a historic putt. Other stand-out moments include winning the Irish Open, the Kenya Open and two senior British Opens. He also had several great victories in America, such as the State Farm Senior Classic, near Baltimore, after beating Bruce Fleisher by one stroke. And he won in America for a second time in mid-August 1999 at the Foremost Insurance Championship, near Grand Rapids.

There are other great Irish pro golfers, like McDowell, Eamonn Darcy and Philip Walton. Ronan Rafferty would be well up on my list also. But winning a major is the calling card.

Another great pro who stands out is Harry Bradshaw, who won the Canada Cup in Mexico with Christy O'Connor Senior. Des Smith, a wonderful player, is also on my list of all-time favourites. He was able to play all the shots and play them well. He played in all the top competitions, including the Ryder Cup, and was playing right up until his fifties as a senior.

If you were to ask me for my favourite amateur golfers I would put Joe Carr on top of the list, without a doubt. Joe's son Roddy also played in the Walker Cup. A close second would be Tom Craddock, who was a beautiful player, an absolute gem of a player. He also played in the Walker Cup. David Feherty was a good player too. He is now a commentator in America. He's a funny man.

One of the greatest golfers ever was born in Dublin; unfortunately, it was Dublin, Texas, so we cannot count him on our list of great Irish golfers! Ben Hogan is one of only five golfers to have won all four major championships (the others are Tiger Woods, Gary Player, Gene Sarazen and Jack Nicklaus). Hogan was probably the smartest and most concise iron-player in the history of golf. He survived a terrible car crash, with horrendous injuries, and there was a distinct chance that he would never walk again. They thought it highly unlikely that he would play golf again, but he did both, and he came back and won championships again. Then he entered the British Open, which is open house for everyone, particularly the best of the Americans. He played it in Carnoustie in 1953, his first and only appearance at the oldest major of them all. He must have been something else, because he won the British Open—the only golfer in history who held a 100 per cent record in the British Open: he played in one and he won one. I never met Hogan, and I would love to have met him.

AUGUSTA MASTERS

Picking the most prestigious golf course in the world as my favourite is a no-brainer. Anyone who has ever stood over a golf ball or ever watched the game on television and heard the legendary names of Palmer, Nicklaus and Tiger would have wished for a visit to the famous Augusta National in Georgia.

It's here where, for the second week of every April, players assemble for the playing of the Masters. It might have the reputation of being the greatest golf event, but it's actually the youngest of golf's four majors, and yet it is the only one that is hosted by the same club every year. In every sense, Augusta is a beautiful venue and is all the more special when it hosts the Masters tournament, because it's here you'll see the *crème de la crème,* as only top players qualify for it. There is hardly an unknown player in the Masters.

But the real star of the Masters is the course itself, an oasis of tranquillity among the Georgia plains. Green is the only colour you'll see here: all the buildings are green, and even the scoreboards. The only place that isn't sparkling green is the sand bunkers.

Let me talk you through from the beginning of a fabulous visit to this number 1 class event. You begin with breakfast on the veranda on the terrace of the Partridge Inn Hotel. It really feels like you could be on the set of *Gone with the Wind,* with the trellis, balconies, the old-style ceiling air coolers, and the service so mannerly and classy. You won't be rushed. When breakfast is finished they have their own mini-bus to bring you to the course. Talk about a *different class*!

The main gate to the course is on the Washington Road. Once inside that gate you will be in one of the very special places and will feel privileged. The avenue leading to the clubhouse is called Magnolia Lane, and it's lined with trees on each side with the famous sixty magnolias stretching 150 yards. When you reach the fountain you've come to the clubhouse, which is called the Founders' Circle. Inside it there are two plaques (in the fountain itself), one dedicated to Bobby Jones and the other to Clifford Roberts, the two founders of the club.

Walk around the corner and you will see a replica of the clubhouse, with every little perfect minute detail of it there. That is near the putting green. You are just bowled over by the whole place. The souvenir shop is fantastic: they have everything in it. And then there is the media centre, and then there is the famous big oak tree, which is alive and growing on the putting green, which, of course, is pristine.

The whole place is pristine. You think that everybody there is somebody.

The funny thing is that at this stage you haven't seen a tee, a green, or a golfer, and the best is yet to come. On the course you will come across Rae's Creek, which is a little stream that runs in front of an original house on the Savannah River owned by John Rae and is naturally out of bonds to us mere spectators.

Then there is the famous Amen Corner, which was so named by a writer called Herbert Warren Wind, who wrote about golf in particular. It is a very tricky corner, where you come down by the tenth and then you have the eleventh and twelfth and thirteenth, and if you perform badly there your chances of winning the Masters evaporate. He decided to call it Amen Corner one time after watching Arnold Palmer playing. He was in trouble, and he played a second ball until the other was deemed by rule to be in play or out of play. So while they were waiting for all that to happen Wind called it Amen Corner.

All the holes in Augusta are named after flowers or shrubs, because the land was formerly an orchard and a flower garden. The three holes on Amen Corner are White Dogwood, Golden Bell and Dahlia, which is probably the most common flower on the course, I think.

If you are ever lucky enough to get a badge for the Masters in Augusta you have to be physically fit to tackle the eighteen beautiful holes. You see it on television and it looks hunky-dory, but there are a lot of ups and downs on the course—some flats, some climbs that can be vicious and tiring to navigate.

There are three famous bridges on the course, each of which is named after a famous Masters golfer: Sarazen on the fifteenth, the Hogan Bridge on the twelfth, and the Nelson Bridge on the thirteenth.

The green jacket is symbolic of the Masters, with the winner getting the green jacket every year. It was first presented in 1949 to Sam Snead, who would have been one of the first golfers I ever interviewed, funnily enough. The winner is allowed to take it home for one year, and then it is returned and is hung in the club with the other green jackets of the winners of all the previous Masters.

They say the most difficult sports event to get access to is the Masters in Augusta. No money is taken at the gate: you just can't walk up and pay in. There is no admission unless you have a badge. How do you get a badge? You have to apply for a badge, except the list is closed, and there is now a waiting-list for the waiting-list! If a family have a badge they keep it in the family.

How do people from here get badges? There is one way: if you rent a house near the course and they have badges they leave the badges for the relevant days in a jug on the hall table. The family know you are going to take the badges, and you take them without asking.

Out on the course the security people who look after it look at the badges, so you must wear your badge at all times. They can't check everybody, but they can carry out spot checks; and all the badges are numbered and cross-referenced. You are warned not to switch your badge with anybody or to give it to anybody who is not properly credited to wear it, and at any time they can stop you, and if your name doesn't match the coded list they will confiscate the badge and you are escorted out of the premises, never to return, they say.

They will obviously ask you how you got the badge, and if you tell them you stole it you are in trouble, and if you say that it was there in the rented house and you took it then that is also stealing and you are also in trouble. If you say you were given it, then those people will be wiped off the list and they won't get any more badges.

Even working for the media might not get you in, as they are also oversubscribed. I used to get there every year. Back in 1974 I was given the opportunity to play the course, but I had to turn it down. They had said they were going to give the press the opportunity to play the course on the Monday after the Masters. We would be playing from the same positions, the tees and the flags would all be in the same place. Anyone interested was to sign up for it; sure everyone signed up. My name came out of the hat, but I had to turn it down, because I was doing a European Cup match for television on the Wednesday, and this would have been on the Monday, and I couldn't get a flight that would bring me from Augusta to Atlanta and then to the match in Rotterdam. No matter how desperate I was to play the course, I just couldn't take a chance, so I reluctantly turned it down. I have no regrets about that.

———

Funny the way life turns out: my son Paul got to play the course shortly before he died from the incurable muscle-wasting illness motor neurone disease. It was one of his lifelong dreams to visit the place, and his friends managed to swing it for him. Now, you simply cannot play Augusta or get into Augusta: you simply have no chance, unless you are someone like the president of the United States; but somehow they arranged it all with a member of the club.

By this time Paul was in a wheelchair. He didn't realise that he was actually going to get inside as his friends drove their car down to Magnolia Lane to meet their contact. An excited Paul couldn't believe he was there and was asking if they thought he could get in. You can only imagine the surprise when he was told they were expecting him and they brought him up to the clubhouse.

Paul was then asked if he would like to play on the course, but he replied that he couldn't play, because at this stage he had lost most of the power in his arms. He was told they would get him a cart and clubs and get a caddy and go around with him. He actually played the whole eighteen holes in Augusta. With all the strength he could muster, he was just able to stand to take the shot and then sit down again. He was able to swing the clubs a bit, and he got a par 3 at the sixteenth, which is a famous par 3. It's a hole that makes and breaks players at the Masters itself.

As it turns out, I prefer that Paul got to play it rather than me.

Chapter 11 ∽

IRISH OLYMPIC HEROES—
THE FIRST TEN

There have been only six Irish men and women who have won gold medals in the entire history of the Olympic Games. I think anybody who wins an Olympic event cannot be overrated. Only two of these great Irish athletes have won two or more gold medals, and that's Pat O'Callaghan, who holds the distinction of winning Ireland's first gold medal as an independent state, and Michelle Smith.

1. MICHELLE SMITH

For my money, Smith has to be miles ahead as our greatest Olympian athlete ever, thanks to her three gold medals and one bronze at the 1996 Atlanta Games. That is a fantastic haul.

I know there could be controversy over placing her at the top of my list, but the facts are that Michelle won those three gold medals, and she is still in the record books. People like to forget that she wasn't stripped of her medals at all. If they knew for a fact that she had done wrong she would have been stripped of her medals by now. She has to be the greatest, despite the fact that she doesn't get a bloody mention here in Ireland. It's almost like committing a mortal sin if you mention her in Ireland, so I will mention her. Her medals are there, and that is a fact.

I did get some grief over what I wrote about her in my last book, *Memory Man*. I was asked many times, How could I defend a drug-user? And I would say, first of all, she is not a drug-user, and she never tested positive once during those Olympic Games. I believe she didn't take any illegal substances, but I find people laugh and try to make out I'm naïve for defending her.

Yes, she was caught, but people again fail to remember, or simply choose to ignore the fact, that she was out of competition when they found the sample to have been tampered with.

I had a book of results at home, and I took it out one day and I examined one of the events in which she had won a gold medal, and I asked one of my daughters, 'Have a look there at all those winners and tell me what you can see.' She said that all she could see was that those who had won the event before Michelle had all won it in a faster time than she had. I asked my daughter whether she thought then they had been taking something. She replied, 'No, but everyone believes it in Michelle's case, because she had improved so much.'

Yes, she had improved under the guidance of her husband; but the fact remains that she won in a time that wouldn't have got her first over the finishing line in the previous four Olympics.

I knew Michelle, and she was justifiably very annoyed at how she was treated, and can you honestly blame her? She is still the champion; she has never been defrocked. Yet she is constantly snubbed, instead of being lauded for her momentous achievements. A case in point is how she wasn't even asked to carry the Olympic flame when it arrived on our shores during the build-up to the London 2012 Games. It's a crying shame, because having the Olympic torch here is the closest we will ever come to hosting the Games.

I was at the Mansion House in the late 1980s or early 90s on the day it was mentioned that Ireland was going to apply to host the Olympics. Now, what do you say to that type of Walter Mitty stuff? Think about it. What do you do for hotels? We are bad enough. I think in future there will be no Olympic Games anywhere other than in a massive city like London, Rio or Sydney. It will have to be a big city that can handle all the logistical nightmares. We are big at heart, but that's about it.

The biggest things we have had here were the UEFA Cup final and the Rugby Cup final. But don't forget that every year we have 82,000 people in Croke Park, twice a year for the two All-Ireland finals. They are the big events. That's a fact.

As I said before in defence of Michelle Smith, she later studied for the bar and finished in the top handful and is now a practising barrister. Tell me this: did she take something to make her better at that? I keep repeating myself; but she took all the appropriate tests at the Olympics, and not one of the results showed any trace of anything illegal.

The timings are a fact. Every four years there is a progression: if you do it in a minute and ten seconds this year you will find that, come Rio 2016, somebody will do it in a minute and eight seconds, and it just slowly gets better. But the four people who won it before Michelle were all faster than her!

In previous years she would have been lucky if she won all bronze and no gold, and she would not have been vilified.

2. PAT O'CALLAGHAN

Moving on, Pat O'Callaghan would be my second all-time greatest Irish Olympian. Everybody thought he was going over to the 1928 Olympics in Amsterdam, along with his older brother, Con, to make up the numbers. Nobody was giving him a chance of winning in the hammer-throwing category. But he won Ireland's first gold that year, and repeated this success in Los Angeles in 1932 by winning on the same day that Bob Tisdall won.

In 1936 he was probably at his best, so they say. But there was a row with the athletics associations, and there was no team sent from Ireland to the Olympics. Maybe he would have won a third medal, but we can't talk about what might have been. Nobody can take away the fact that he's our first gold-medal hero.

Technically, he isn't the first Irish-born winner, because there was a fella named John Hayes who won the marathon in London in 1908 for America, but he was actually from Co. Tipperary. But sure back then everybody was Irish!

In the Courthouse in Nenagh there is a statue with three Olympians on it: Pat McGrath (for the USA), Bob Tisdall and John Hayes, who all won gold medals and are all originally from that area. Tisdall was the only one not to be born in Ireland, but he represented Ireland and won a gold medal. Can anybody guess where he was born? It's a good pub-quiz question. He was born in Sri Lanka.

Incidentally, a man with an Irish name won the first gold medal in the modern Olympics. James Connolly won the triple jump, which itself is an Irish event: it's the old hop, step and jump.

Anyway, back to the late great O'Callaghan. When I was doing a little series for radio called 'Where Are They Now?' I would always carry the recording equipment in my car. One day I was driving down to Co. Tipperary, where O'Callaghan had his practice as a GP. He would show the sick children his medals, which hung on the wall of his office.

I said to my wife, who was with me at the time, that I wanted to call in to him during our journey. Of course she told me I couldn't just call in on someone unless I had an arrangement with them. But I called in anyway, and he invited us in and told me he would love to do an interview. So we sat down and had tea and scones, and he did a whole piece for me. We did the whole programme there and then. I acknowledge that it was cheek in the extreme, but I didn't do it cheekily; the phrase now would be I doorstepped him. He was a funny man.

3. RON DELANY

The third name on my list is Ron Delany, who won the Blue Riband, if you like—the 1,500 metres, the metric mile—which is still held in high esteem as the main event to win in athletics. If you had a choice of an event to win and you wanted to become the sprint champion or the 1,500-metre champ you could either become Usain Bolt or Taoufik Makhloufi, who won the 1,500 in London.

If you want to become the sprint champion you have to have talent—that's a given, because if you don't have the talent you can do all the work you like and it doesn't matter a damn. Delany showed the world his talent when he won in Melbourne in 1956.

Delany went to Villanova University in Philadelphia. He was a wonderful runner there and enjoyed big success over there. I would love to have seen Delany at Villanova, where he was coached by a legendary figure, Jumbo Elliott, who also trained Eamonn Coghlan.

Delany also had a big success at the indoor running there. He won loads of indoor events, long before Coghlan was named Chairman of the Boards. Outdoors he was also a wonderful runner, and he peaked when you needed him to peak. If you want to win the Derby you run well that day; if you want to win the Grand National you have to jump well on that day; and, by God, Delany did it when the chips were down. On that day alone he has to be away up in the pecking order, no doubt about it. He would be rated as better than Eamonn Coghlan, because he won an Olympic medal; but I would have Coghlan away up there too.

As I pointed out earlier, Delany was trained by the fantastic Jumbo Elliott at Villanova. Jumbo had Delany repeatedly practising running and breaking the tape, and running harder and breaking the tape. Why? Only one man breaks the tape—the winner—and he was being trained to be the winner.

At that time, in 1956, you touched the tape with your chest to break it and signify you were first across the line. You must remember that this was before it all became digitally controlled. The first man to breast the tape was the winner. Elliott had him running as hard as he could and breaking the tape, because then you would learn how to win.

Some people didn't want Delany to go to the Olympics at all, because he lost a couple of races in Lansdowne Road to Brian Hewson of England, who was also going to be in the Olympics and indeed was in the twelve-man final with Delany. There was a fear that maybe Delany wouldn't get on well. Some of us had faith in him, but I wasn't in Melbourne. If I could turn back the clock and be there I would. I listened to it on the BBC. A man called Rex Alston was doing the commentary on the crackly old radio, and I remember one of his phrases was 'Delany of Éire,' and that used to annoy some of the lads, who would have preferred if Delany didn't run at all if that's what he was going to be called. It touched a nerve with Irish people. If you're going to use 'Éire' then all the others should be used also, such as Italia and Deutschland, etc.

Withdrawn From Stock
Dublin Public Libraries

When Delany won the gold medal there was a great reaction, but you also have to remember this was the pre-television era, so it was much later before anyone saw it.

Despite losing those pre-Olympic races, I remember being confident that Delany was going to win—not just through Irish blind faith but I thought he was a dead cert for it.

The astonishing thing about him is that in coming to the closing stages of the race Delany was towards the back of the field; he wasn't last but he was next to last of twelve runners in it, and they were covered by no more than 10 or 12 yards. Hewson and Merv Lincoln of Australia were leading, and everyone was in with a shout. There was no bell for the last lap, because the official either forgot about it or dozed off or something; but if you were a real athlete you would be counting your laps anyway.

At that stage he was well at the back, and then he began to give chase in an amazing performance. He was in the so-called box—he was boxed in—and something else Jumbo Elliott taught him: if you are ever in a box in a race never lose your rag or get upset, just think clearly about how everybody is moving, nobody is standing still stopping your progress, just be patient and you will get your opportunity. And he did. He was coming up on a man called Gunnar Nielsen. The great Danish runner felt or saw him coming, and he moved slightly aside to allow Delany up on the inside. At 300 metres he started going, and certainly at 120 metres he started picking them off one by one. It was an electrifying sight— wonderful stuff; and you would wonder how he was able to do that.

Well, I will tell you how he was able to do it. He ran the last lap in 53.8 seconds, he ran the last 200 metres in 25.6, at the end of a 1,500-metre race, and he ran the last 100 metres in about 12.85 seconds. It is just an astonishing speed at the end of such a long run. When he hit the finishing line Delany dropped to his knees from exhaustion. John Landy of Australia—who finished third and was one of the great milers of all time—bent down to help him. They were great friends, and still are great friends. A man called Klaus Richtzenhain of East Germany was second.

Delany was well known for his so-called kick, but by God he kicked that day, the greatest kick he ever produced: he kicked on the last lap, kicked on the last 300, the last 200, the last 100. It was Olympic running at its absolute peak.

The Blue Riband of the Olympic Games was the 1,500 metres, and it still is regarded as the event to win, and he won it, and nobody from here has come within an ass's roar of it since.

I think Delany knew he was going to win it, and he would also say that everybody else running would have known he was going to win it. Sadly, he never did it again. But he did win bronze four years later in Stockholm. In fact only one runner ever got gold medals in the 1,500-metre race in two consecutive Olympics, and that is Sebastian Coe, who did it in the 1,500 metres in Moscow and Los Angeles.

4. BOB TISDALL

My candidate for fourth place is Bob Tisdall, who won gold in the 400-metres hurdle and broke a world record in the process, which was not recognised, because he hit a hurdle during the event. This rule was changed because of the Tisdall incident.

Tisdall, who was born in Sri Lanka, was really a rookie at the 400-metres hurdle event and had only run a handful of races before the Olympics in 1932 in Los Angeles. There is a lovely photograph that was taken diagonally across the track as the first four athletes are about to cross the finishing line. Tisdall is winning, so therefore he is the Olympic Champion; the man in second place was the prior Olympic champion; the man who was third was the Olympic champion four years before that; again the other person was the champion of the Games after that! Just think about it: four Olympic champions!

5. MICHAEL CARRUTH

We've won more medals in boxing than in any of the other disciplines, with 16 of our total of 28 coming from pugilists. But the stand-out for me was when the Dubliner Michael Carruth won Ireland's first gold medal in boxing at the 1992 Barcelona Games.

Knocked out in his first attempt at Olympic glory in 1988, this southpaw came back more determined than ever four years later to win gold in the welterweight division. Amazingly, his victory was the first time Ireland earned a gold medal since Ronnie Delany, all the way back in 1956.

6. KATIE TAYLOR

Katie was the unbeaten best in the world at the time of the Olympics; she had four European Union Championships, five European Championships and four world titles. She then became the first female boxer in her weight to win gold at the Olympics in London in 2012. Without fail, when it came to the fights that mattered she has consistently gone out and won them in style.

The boxer she met in the Olympic final was the best boxer apart from herself in the tournament. It was a difficult match. They had met before, and they knew what to expect of each other. Katie was a really wonderful winner, who also handled it very well, and sure she packed the place out. It was a very special Olympic day for the entire country when she won Ireland's first gold medal since Michelle Smith's in 1996.

After hearing that Katie would be meeting her Russian foe in the final she admitted that it would be a 50-50 fight. 'The pressure is always going to be on both boxers, as we are both boxing for gold,' Katie said.

The usually confident-looking Katie was visibly apprehensive before the start of the Olympic final against her Russian counterpart, Sofya Ochigava, who had once beaten the Irish world champion. 'I was so nervous; it was the most nervous I've been for a fight. I had a knot in my stomach all day. It was hard to relax, I couldn't even eat all day. But when I got in there it was just like any other contest,' Katie admitted.

Her father, Peter, had spent the night before the final repeatedly watching the Russian boxer's semi-final against the Brazilian Adriana Araújo. It was a very tight bout, and the Russian was somewhat lucky to come away with a flattering score of 17-11.

It was a tough if somewhat unspectacular final—thanks to the Russian southpaw's defensive spoiling tactics and her ability to slow the

Arkle, ridden by the great Pat Taaffe, the best steeplechaser of all time. (© *Getty Images*)

Brian O'Driscoll, simply the best Irish rugby player I have seen. It's hard to compare the professional with the amateur era, but O'Driscoll's all-round game, both in attack and defence, together with his longevity, places him in a class of his own. (© *INPHO/Colm O'Neill*)

Carl Lewis, the most outstanding all-round athlete of my time. (© *Diane Johnson/ Alamy*)

Two of the genuine greats, Johan Cruyff and Franz Beckenbauer. (© *Getty Images*)

Christy O'Connor Senior (*right*). For two decades he was Ireland's leading professional golfer. (© *Getty Images*)

Different class: Diego Maradona (*right*). (© INTERFOTO/*Alamy*)

Eddy Merckx—not just a favourite of mine but one of the best-loved cyclists ever to ride the Tour de France. (© *Graham Morley Historic Photos/Alamy*)

King Henry. Shefflin has been the best player on the best hurling team I have ever seen. (© *INPHO/ Billy Stickland*)

Golden Bear: Jack Nicklaus. (© *Getty Images*)

Big Jack (*right*). Was there ever an Englishman who made Ireland happier? (© *David Maher* /SPORTSFILE)

Michael Schumacher, the most relentlessly competitive driver in the history of Formula One. (© *Getty Images*)

The Kerry football team of the late 1970s and early 80s was possibly the best ever, and you could make a good case for saying that Jack O'Shea was the best player on the best team. (© *INPHO/Billy Stickland*)

Jimmy Barry Murphy was a star and a winner as hurler, footballer and manager, one of the truly outstanding GAA personalities. (© *INPHO/Billy Stickland*)

John Giles with someone I know. Not only was he the finest Irish footballer of his generation, he is beyond any question the best analyst of the game in the English-speaking world. (© *David Maher/ SPORTSFILE*)

The greatest: Muhammad Ali. There is no more to be said. (© *Keystone Pictures USA/Alamy*)

Mary Peters (*left*) is the finest all-round woman athlete that Ireland has produced. Here she comes out of the blocks at the start of the 200-metre event in the women's pentathlon at the 1972 Munich Olympics. (© *Getty Images*)

By common consensus, the greatest footballer of our time, Pelé. (© *Keystone Pictures USA/Alamy*)

Peter Canavan was not just an outstanding footballer: he was the key forward in the successful Tyrone team of the mid-2000s. (© INPHO/*James Meehan*)

One of the toughest men in a brutally tough sport: Seán Kelly. (© *AFP*/*Getty Images*)

Tony Hanahoe (*left*) was captain and the beating heart of Kevin Heffernan's Dublin team of the 1970s. They revived Gaelic football in the capital at a time when it was under threat, and they played a brilliant, open brand of football. (© *Connolly Collection/* SPORTSFILE)

Mick O'Connell, a true legend of Kerry football. There was never a more aesthetically pleasing player. (© *Ray McManus/* SPORTSFILE)

One of the great images in all Irish sport: Ronnie Delany wins the Blue Riband 1,500 metres at the 1956 Olympics in Melbourne. (© *Getty Images*)

Stephen Roche (*centre*), so far the only Irish winner of the Tour de France. (© *AFP/Getty Images*)

No golfer was ever more loved than Seve Ballesteros. His cavalier shot-making was without equal; he took outrageous risks and got away with them; the crowds adored him. Tragically, he died young. (© *Sport Picture Library/ Alamy*)

Tiger Woods: perhaps the most outrageously gifted golf talent of them all. (© *Getty Images*)

fight down, coupled with a counter-attacking style that definitely troubled Katie. The two boxers cautiously circled each other in the first round, which ended in a 2-2 draw—giving credence to Katie's view that it would be a 50-50 bout.

The judges inexplicably awarded Katie only one point in the second round, which went in the Russian's favour by a single point, to give her a 4-3 advantage.

The tension was palpable in the arena as apprehensive Irish supporters began to fear that perhaps it wasn't going to be Katie's day. But a determined Katie didn't disappoint in the third round, when she showed her world class by comprehensively outpunching her opponent. The fans erupted when they realised she had won that round 4-1, which meant that she was going into the last round with a 7-5 advantage.

The final round was tense and too close to call. The Russian finally opened up and threw herself forward in a last-ditch effort to pull back the score; but it was too little, too late. As with the first round, the judges deemed it a 3-3 draw, but this was more than enough to give Katie a well-deserved 10-8 victory.

While Katie anxiously waited for the result to be confirmed I did my best to assure anxious viewers back home that the Irish boxer had achieved her dream of winning the Olympic gold medal. 'Surely the gold medal is on its way back to Bray,' I maintained.

Who will ever forget Katie Taylor winning the boxing gold medal to an uproarious reception and a standing ovation, in the true sense of the word? She received a long-winded standing ovation from friend and foe (she didn't seem to have any foes, though), standing ovation upon standing ovation, and they seemed to be applauding for ten minutes.

I think it was the greatest reception I have ever seen for any performer in the boxing ring, and I have been doing the boxing for forty-seven years now. It was certainly the best an Irish athlete has ever received.

Ireland won five medals (one gold, one silver and three bronze) at the 2012 Olympics, four of which came from boxing, with the fifth in horse-jumping; but what we will remember most is how the entire country rejoiced as Katie danced around the ring with joy after she had won what was only Ireland's ninth gold medal since independence. She was now in the company of only six other Irish gold-medallists: Pat O'Callaghan, Bob Tisdall, Ronnie Delany, Michael Carruth and Michelle Smith.

It was poetic justice that this trailblazer in women's boxing won that first gold medal in boxing, because the Olympic Committee had been persuaded to permit women's boxing in the Games after some of its members were impressed from watching Katie in an exhibition match.

Katie could now even surpass her own childhood dream of winning that single Olympic gold by winning again at Rio in 2014. It's hard to imagine anybody beating her. She truly is a *different class*.

7. JOHN TREACY

In seventh place of my all-time great Irish Olympic moments would have to be John Treacy's silver medal, which was as good as gold as far as I'm concerned, because nobody had anticipated it—apart from the man himself.

At the 1984 Olympic Games in Los Angeles I was invited to a party, and I had a memorable conversation that night with the legendary runner, who certainly deserves the accolade of being in a *different class*. He had just completed one event at the Olympics and was now gearing up for the marathon, which was to be his first one, believe it or not. We were huddled up in the corner and out of earshot of most of the revellers.

'I see you're entered in it,' I said, referring to the marathon.

'I'm going to run too. I've been working up to it, and if this wall that you hit at twenty miles—and I don't know what that's like, because I've never run that far—is not as bad as they tell me and I reach it and manage to get over it, keep an eye out for me. Are you doing the commentary? Watch out for little John, because if I get over that part I will be in the running.'

He then asked me not to say that on air, as it would sound presumptuous of him. I assured him that I wouldn't. However, during the end of the race Treacy was true to his word as he dashed into the stadium along with Carlos Lopes of Portugal and Charlie Spedding of Great Britain. Lopes broke away and was clearly going to win it; so the race for the silver medal was between Treacy and Spedding. Second place would have been a record for an Irish athlete in the marathon. I remember being on air doing the marathon in which Jerry Kiernan finished ninth, which alone would have been a record performance by an Irishman.

After Lopes won, the other two were shoulder to shoulder to battle it out for silver. Could Ireland possibly get the silver? It was in that time that Treacy became a national hero and a national property. As they ran side by side I was working out in my mind who won what and where—all the statistics involving Irish athletes—and I knew that Ireland had won twelve Olympic medals up to that point. I began wondering to myself, while still doing the commentary, how long it would take me to get out those twelve names. I thought I could do it in about twelve seconds. So when the boys hit the last bend, with about 110 metres to go, I began to list off the previous Irish winners. As Treacy was victoriously crossing the line I was saying, 'And for the thirteenth time, Treacy wins a medal for Ireland.'

I am always linked to that event, and Treacy has told me that he goes to functions and fellas say to him, 'Where's Jimmy?' as though he couldn't appear without me being there. Likewise, I would have fellas asking me if Treacy was with me.

The chat we had at that party came true, which just shows you the sort of athlete he was: he knew if he had the guts to get past the wall he was in the running for a medal.

8. KENNETH EGAN

It speaks volumes about the calibre of Irish boxing that eight of those I have selected as my all-time greatest Irish Olympians are boxers. In fact going through the sport history books I could have included several more boxers, such as the Derryman Charlie Nash, a lightweight who was a beautiful stylist and a terrific puncher. Nash was a great Irish champion, who did us proud in the Olympics in 1972 and went on to have a good career as a pro. Likewise, fans of the Belfast-born fighter Michael Conlan could justifiably feel he deserves a place in my list because of his momentous achievement in bringing home a bronze medal in the flyweight division from London in 2012.

Unfortunately I can only select a top-twenty list, and I would be doing a great disservice if the name of Kenneth Egan didn't make the cut. He is one of the finest Irish amateur boxers ever to grace a boxing ring. Here is a true champ who has the distinction of winning ten consecutive Irish titles, making him the only Irishman to do so. Yes, there is one other boxer to win ten Irish titles, but he didn't achieve ten consecutively. As Egan explains, 'I won ten senior titles before that; it's a record in itself. There is only one other guy who has ten senior titles, Jim O'Sullivan, but he hasn't got them consecutively. I have ten in a row—my own little record; but I'd love to get that number 11.'

Sadly, he didn't win that eleventh medal but he did manage to make it to thirteen finals before hanging up his gloves, which is a record in itself. He showed what he was made of in Beijing by getting all the way to the final of the light-heavy division and winning silver, beating many fine opponents on the journey. He still believes he won the gold, losing out to a biased panel of judges who favoured the local Chinese hero. 'I didn't actually win the silver: I lost the gold! I was robbed. I won the fight on points; but I'm not going to make a big song and dance about it. If I'd been offered silver at the start of the Games I would have taken it. I got to the podium; that's the dream I always had,' he says.

He also has three gold medals in the EU amateur championships and several bronzes. He is certainly a *different class*.

9. WAYNE McCULLOUGH

A few hours before Michael Carruth's famous victory at the 1992 Olympic Games, Wayne McCullough had to settle for silver after losing on points to the Cuban Joel Casamayor, who went on to win several titles as a pro fighter. McCullough was excellent, and he would have been a close contender for the boxer of the Olympics. There is an award called the Val Barker Trophy, and he probably would have got it if he won gold. He was outstanding in Barcelona, and I know from my insider knowledge that he was close to getting the boxer of the championship award. He probably lost it in the semi-final match against the North Korean, which was called the Hammer Match—that was when he damaged his eye, and it has never been properly cured; he still doesn't have the feeling back in it.

That fight for the gold medal was very close, but Wayne had that eye injury from the semi-final. The injury was at the top of the cheekbone, under the eye, and it had got to the stage where he had no feeling in that area. Every time he was hit in the final there was blood coming from the injured area and spurting out. But it didn't deter him from fighting on.

Another thing that made McCullough special was when he went pro and he won the world title in Japan. It was unknown for a stranger to win a world title professionally in Japan, unheard of that any foreigner could do it. As an amateur he was one of the greatest boxers we ever had. He would be right up there, except in the matter of winning championship titles. So, unfortunately, he doesn't get a higher ranking in my list.

10. JOHN JOE NEVIN

Another silver medallist who did his country proud is the Mullingar man John Joe Nevin, who proved how much of a brilliant boxer he is by winning the European Championship in style in June 2013. There might be a possibility that he doesn't get enough respect because he is from the Travelling community. There is no discrimination in the media—definitely not. I know when I am doing the commentary, as I have done for all these years, his background or anything else does not come into it: I genuinely don't care. I know the fella well and only work on his performances. Why should I be biased? Sadly, I don't think he is accepted in the public eye as he deserves to be. There is still a lot of discrimination here.

He should have won the final at London in 2012 against his English opponent, Luke Campbell, whose grandfather, funnily enough, was an Irish boxing champ. And he was well capable of winning it; perhaps it was nerves that undid him. He is the only Irish boxer to win two world medals: two bronze in the World Amateur Championship and an Olympic medal. He also won gold and silver at the EU Amateur Championships.

I think he has the potential to win gold in Rio, because he has fought all the best and he has beaten most of them.

And I trust that the remarkable Billy Walsh will be in charge in Rio. His know-how and personality are embroidered into the now long sequence of Irish boxing successes.

Chapter 12 ∾

IRISH OLYMPIC HEROES— THE FINAL TEN

T he final ten on my list include some worthy Olympic medallists and some of those who, despite being a *different class* in their sporting field, failed to live up to the expectation. But there's no disputing that they are all outstanding Irish sports heroes. So, here is the list of those who make the cut.

11 AND 12. DAVID WILKINS AND JAMIE WILKINSON

These two won silver medals in the boat together, the Flying Dutchman class, at the Moscow Olympics in 1980. That event took place in the waters outside Tallinn, the capital city of Estonia. I was in Moscow and the reaction was very good. David Wilkins was at five Olympic Games, a span of sixteen years, inclusive.

13. FRED TIEDT

Fred was a wonderful boxer who won a silver medal at the 1956 Olympics in Melbourne. He was one of four boxers to win medals for Ireland at that particular Games. For the record, the others were the Drogheda man Anthony Byrne, who won bronze in the lightweight division, and two Belfast men, John Caldwell and Freddie Gilroy, who I will discuss later on.

Tiedt lost the final of the welterweight division in a split decision against a Romanian, Nicolae Linca. It was a different scoring system back then, but if they had done it the way it's done today and added all the individual scores of the judges together Tiedt would have won it; but unfortunately it wasn't done like that. You had five judges, and you voted for who you thought would win it, and it was 3-2, against Tiedt, but the cumulative scores were in the Dubliner's favour.

14. DARREN SUTHERLAND

A man who was capable of winning gold—and I was there to see him up close at the Beijing Games in 2008—was the late Darren Sutherland. He was well capable of winning the whole Olympic championship but came back with a bronze medal. I think he was the best in it that year.

He had a determination to win an Olympic medal, and he won it in super style, and maybe his mind was telling him, 'Now you have your Olympic medal,' and perhaps he then subconsciously took his foot off the pedal, so to speak.

In the semi-final he met James DeGale, a British boxer, and he had beaten DeGale four or five times before this bout. I thought he should have won and was well capable of winning.

I think there are still question marks over his suicide, but I don't think any of us know enough about it. If he was my son I wouldn't have let him turn pro, but he wasn't, so . . .

He was bloody brilliant, and I really think if he was in the next Olympics he would have got that elusive gold.

15. PADDY BARNES

I would describe Paddy Barnes in just one word: brilliant. He is the only Irish boxer to win medals at two Olympic Games, with his bronze in Beijing and bronze in London.

The semi-final in Beijing that he lost was an absolute disgrace. There was no doubt the other man beat Barnes, but there *was* doubt over the score, because Barnes never got a single point, with the judges giving a home-town decision of 15-0 to the Chinese boxer Zou Shiming. I don't know if it was fixed or whether the judges were just blind or something.

Barnes was unlucky in London, in that he was beaten by the unbeatable Chinese man, who was the reigning world and Olympic champion. He was only beaten on a count back, with the judges' originally giving them both a score of 15 points. The whole Irish team in Beijing were beaten by the eventual gold-medallists.

But Barnes is another fighter who could go on to Rio with a realistic chance of winning another medal to add to his two bronze medals from the Olympics, along with his gold from the Commonwealth Games and gold and silver from the European Amateur Championships.

16 AND 17. FREDDIE GILROY AND JOHN CALDWELL

The Belfast-born Freddie Gilroy was an excellent boxer who won bronze at the 1956 Olympics in Melbourne at bantamweight. He won British, Commonwealth and European titles in his career. He was also a very good pro and fought for the world title against Alphonse Halimi but sadly lost on points. Halimi later lost to another Belfastman and also an Olympic bronze medallist in Australia, John Caldwell, who was the first Irishman since Rinty Monaghan in 1948 to win a world title.

Gilroy and Caldwell participated in what is regarded as one of the greatest fights ever in Ireland. Caldwell won that fight, but it would be difficult to separate these two, no matter how you would do it, as they were both brilliant.

18. CIAN O'CONNOR

There's no doubt that Cian O'Connor is a controversial figure after being deprived of his gold medal when his horse, Waterford Crystal, later tested positive for a prohibited substance at the 2004 Games in Athens.

Despite the ruling by the Fédération Equestre Internationale that O'Connor didn't deliberately attempt to affect the performance of the horse, he seemed to go overnight from a worshipped national figure to public enemy number 1—in the eyes of the media anyway. I think people deserve a second chance. Without trying to sound funny, I really think there's an argument for banning the horse, because there is no use banning the rider, as it's always possible that it was somebody else who doped the horse.

He redeemed himself all those years later at London in 2012 when he won a bronze medal in the individual show-jumping competition with his horse Blue Lloyd.

19. EAMONN COGHLAN

He never won a medal at the Olympics, but Eamonn Coghlan deserves a special mention because he was robbed in Moscow, when it was discovered years later that one of the runners who beat him had taken illegal drugs. I have my suspicions about some of the others from that race too.

It originally looked as if Eamonn, known as the Chairman of the Boards because of his great success on indoor tracks, was going to win a medal at the 1976 Games, after he had won the heats and the semifinal. But he failed to live up to his promise in the final itself. He is the first to admit that he ran a 'stupid tactical race' on that occasion. He won all his heats in the 1,500 metres. He was flying and he was just caught out; he was positioned nearly perfectly and was eventually overtaken by John Walker, who was the King of the Road at that time. Walker was just brilliant. He was the first man to run it in less than 3.50 minutes. You are talking about a *different class* there. He was going to win it, and as it turned out he did.

In second place was Ivo van Damme of Belgium, who was essentially an 800-metre runner, so he had the speed. At the best it looked as if Coghlan might get a bronze, and at the very last stride he was pipped to the post for a medal by Paul Wellman of Germany. So he finished fourth, and four years later he was fourth again in the 5,000 metres.

He was destined never to win it. But it's a measure of the man's steely determination that he almost won in Moscow—despite the fact that he came down with a bug two weeks before the race and was 'as sick as a dog' and spent a week in bed. He also ran that race with a stress fracture in his shin-bone, which he told nobody about. In retrospect, he reckons he trained too hard for the race.

Eamonn himself feels that the fatal mistake he made in the race was going into the lead too early. But he almost ran the perfect race: he was everywhere he wanted to be at every particular juncture. But when he pressed the pedal during the last 100 metres nothing happened, and he was overtaken by the eventual winner, the Ethiopian Miruts Yifter, who had been boxed in but was able to sprint ahead when one of his compatriots pulled aside to allow him out. 'I knew I could beat him, but I was just dilapidated. And when I went down the home straight I was just gone,' Coghlan recalls.

We felt he was cheated in Moscow. He did say later that he had a virus, but he never used that as an excuse, and he should have said it really at the time.

Years later Kaarlo Maaninka, who finished second in the 10,000 metres and third in the 5,000 metres, admitted that he had taken dope. He became a 'born-again' Christian, and because of the guilt of winning them he threw his silver and bronze medals into a lake. At the time a number of journalists began to voice their opinion that Coghlan should be getting the bronze medal; but Coghlan himself told a journalist, 'Hold on, lads! I'm not going to go down that road. I wasn't running for a bronze medal, I was running for a gold medal.'

Does he feel hard done by?

'No, I don't. I don't look back with regret. I've had a fantastic life. Somebody has to finish fourth. Roger Bannister—the first man to run a sub-four-minute mile—finished fourth. I was the first man over forty to run a sub-four-minute mile. There are many greats who finished fourth. That's life. You move on.'

And move on he certainly did. He defied all the odds in 1983 by coming back from a career-threatening injury to become the first and only Irish athlete to win gold at the inaugural world championships in Helsinki.

Eamonn—who as a student in America had broken the long-standing European outdoor mile and then broke the world record four years later—also made it into the record books by becoming the first man over forty to run a mile in less than four minutes. So two fourths in the Olympics and one first in the world championship is pretty hot form too.

20. SONIA O'SULLIVAN

Unfortunately she also never won gold at the Olympics, but it would be a crying shame if I didn't mention Sonia O'Sullivan. A great weight of expectation was placed on the shoulders of Sonia to win gold. She wasn't a near-miss in general talent but she was a near-miss on the day, if you know what I mean, at the Sydney Olympics in 2000 when she competed in the 5,000-metre event. She wasn't robbed or anything like that, except that she was beaten by Gabriela Szabo of Romania, and there were some grave drugs reservations about her. But winning silver is better than many other Irish athletes have achieved in many decades.

The day of the medal race she ended up sick and running off the track with diarrhoea. This was her maxima day, but I think she had other days when she could have had her maxima: she was the best Irish runner ever, certainly our best female runner, and she should have won a gold medal. But her cv without an Olympic gold is still impressive: she got gold at the world championship in 1985, three further gold medals at the European Championship, two more gold medals at the world cross-country championship, gold at the Universiade and gold at the Continental Cup. On top of that she has more than half a dozen silver and bronze medals from all these events too.

————

He doesn't make my top twenty list, as he's not an athlete, but a final mention must go to the unsung hero that is Brother Colm O'Connell, based in Kenya as a missionary, who has produced some great athletes. They have come good for him on many occasions, despite living at a high altitude. Also, they have the talent—they always had the talent— and he just happened upon it, by his own admission.

He has produced unbelievable runners, including—for my money— perhaps the greatest track and field achievement ever in the London Games in 2012 with David Rudisha in the 800 metres. From the moment the pistol was fired he just seemed to ease across the ground, as if he had castors on his feet. It was an amazing performance at top speed over the 800 metres. He breasted the finishing line in 1 minute 48.9 seconds, which was a new world record for 800 metres. It was the fastest half mile any of us have ever seen, from a man who has broken several world records already, and he's still only in his early twenties.

He's a wonderful 800-metre runner, and there have been some great ones, such as Alberto Juantorena and Seb Coe, but nobody has ever been in this league, as if he was a power burner without any great effort. He is the best half-miler I have ever seen—a beautiful, beautiful athlete, who is a *different class*.

Amazingly, despite all these great victories, Brother O'Connell is not from an athletic background. What makes him special as a coach, by his own modest admission, is that he's interested in human beings, and he just happened to stumble upon these very special people. It appears to be more than luck when you look at Brother O'Connell's stats as a coach: his runners have collected ten Olympic medals, five of them gold, and twenty-five world championship medals. As far as coaching goes, this brother is certainly in a *different class*. I can't think of any Irish coach, never mind any other top international coach, who even comes close to this extraordinary record.

Chapter 13 ∾

| TOUR DE FORCE

T he biggest annual sports event in the world is the Tour de France. Most people in France see it, and they see it free of charge, for twenty-three days every July, because they can go out onto the roads for miles and miles. It's been going since 1903 without interruption, except during the two world wars.

On average this multi-stage bicycle race is 3,500 kilometres in length. I say 'on average' because sometimes it can be longer, depending on the route chosen in a particular year. In 1988 it actually started in Ireland, and the cyclist who won that year was an Italian named Marco Pantani—aptly nicknamed 'the Pirate', as he was using illegal substances to help him win. But all the same it was special to see it held in Ireland. I had been covering it for about ten years abroad, so for me at least it was special.

Every day the organisers erect a mobile village at the next stage, which is taken down the following morning and the process repeated at the next stage. If you went to the spot a couple of hours after the tour has passed through you would not realise that one of the greatest events in the world had just passed through. I think it is fascinating that here we have a massive sports event, with thousands of people involved— the riders themselves, their rub-down men, managers, agents, advertising people, all the media—and within a couple of hours of departing there is not a sign of this yoke, with the coffee machines and doughnut stands all gone to the next town. It is staged as if there is a permanence about it, but that permanence is only for one day.

The big thing in the Tour de France, which is mind-boggling, is the climbs. Unless you were on them you would not believe that anyone could get over them on a bike. I drove over them and the car would be struggling in first gear, really pushing it. The ones that stand out are Galibier, Tourmalet and Mont Ventoux, which is a bald white mountain with no vegetation at all on it, because the summit is in the middle of the sky. Tragically, that's where the English rider Tommy Simpson died in 1967. He died from an overdose of whatever he had taken, which had an adverse reaction with the scorching heat. He died on the bike, and his last words were essentially, 'Put me back up again!' The drugs probably did it, but what really did it was the height and this fierce hot day. There is a little statue to him there now. There have been almost a dozen fatalities on the gruelling Tour de France.

One of the most spectacular climbs on the tour is Alpe d'Huez, which is truly unbelievable: it is a 13.9 km climb and about 1,860 metres above sea level, an average 7.9 per cent gradient, maximum 11.5 per cent. I've always wondered how the riders can stomach this climb, because of the drop. Not only does it not appear safe but this one can psychologically drain the riders, because the bends are like a hinge, one on top of the other; from one hairpin bend to the next one, they overlap. The bends are all numbered, and I think the numbers do it, because psychologically they play with the mind. Sure you would have to go mad from all the counting! Away up there the riders can see the crowds, and it must surely be daunting knowing that they have to go there.

The great climbers make it, but it is next thing to impossible for the riders who are not good at climbing. I remember we were waiting for Seán Kelly at the finishing line one year, and you could watch them coming the whole way up the mountain. Eventually he arrived, and he was absolutely knackered but with delight on his face. He was in good form, though, and he said, 'Do you know something, Jimmy? Only for you and RTE being here I don't think I would have finished this route today!' It must have been about 80 degrees. He won the green jersey that year. What an astonishing fella Kelly was!

That route is not on every Tour, as they do a new route every year, but it would certainly be between every two and three years, as they try and get around all the famous places. That would be one of the big ones, though.

The Tour de France is made up of three elements, with the winning cyclist getting a jersey for each of these categories: time trials, mountain-climbing (white jersey with red polka dots) and flat-terrain sprints (green jersey). There is also a rainbow jersey for the reigning world champion during the race, and a white jersey for the best performer in the young rider division. Each of them is very important, but everybody will no doubt agree that the most important jersey is the yellow one. A yellow jersey is up for grabs every day and is worn by the overall race leader. But when they started the Tour they didn't have a yellow jersey, and people would wonder, 'Who's leading the race?' You could see them passing by, but sure the fella who is passing by you first on the road is not necessarily the leader. The yellow jersey is awarded to the rider who goes that distance in the shortest possible time, including bonuses. So by wearing the yellow jersey everybody knows who the leader is. At the end of the tour the rider who has won the Tour gets a permanent yellow jersey.

The next most important jersey is the red polka-dot one, awarded to the best climber, which is a different matter altogether. It is a specialist race, called the King of the Mountains. Then you have the sprinters' jersey, which is green and is given to the most consistent rider every day, which is usually a sprinter. Seán Kelly has won that jersey four times, and he is second on the all-time list of holders of it, which is a fantastic achievement. Every day he was up there challenging, except in the mountains.

Our other great rider, Stephen Roche, was brilliant at time-trialling, which was another string to his bow that Kelly didn't have. Yet Kelly's time trial in Carrick-on-Suir is one of the greatest pieces of television ever, when he broke the record. So it's certainly not fair to say that Kelly couldn't time-trial.

The Tour's best cyclist ever was Eddy Merckx, who won all three jerseys in 1969, the only one ever to have done it, and it will never be done again. There is no need for me to hesitate when I rate Eddy the number 1 bike racer. He has won the Tour de France five times, along with Miguel Indurain Larraya, Jacques Anquetil and Bernard Hinault (remember that the drug cheat Lance Armstrong's record of seven wins no longer exists). Eddy also won the Giro d'Italia five times. They are the two grand tours. They are equal in distance and other factors, but the Tour de France was first, so it has the bigger reputation. But they are equally tough tours.

Eddy also won three world titles; he also held the hour record and has more yellow jerseys than any man on earth. He also has more stage jerseys than anyone else, and is the only cyclist ever to hold all three main jerseys. To win all three jerseys in a Tour de France in 1969 was absolutely amazing, because it was never done before and has definitely not been done since. Even if Lance had not been found out he could still not equal Merckx. Merckx could sprint, climb, time-trial: he could do everything. If they were both thirty years old I think Merckx would scalp him.

Who do I reckon is second to Merckx? There were a lot of great cyclists. Perhaps Bernard Hinault of France, but it's very hard to say without Armstrong, who is a self-confessed drug cheat. You'd have to place Stephen Roche on any top five list for the simple fact that he is only the second cyclist in the history of the sport, after Merckx, to win the Triple Crown of Cycling in 1987 by coming first in the Tour de France, the Giro d'Italia and the World Road Race Championship in one sporting calendar year.

Another great Irish cyclist was Shay Elliott from Bray, who was the first Irishman to wear the yellow jersey. We never hear of him now, which is an awful pity. I knew Shay, and he was a brilliant cyclist. He nearly won the world title, but was kind of robbed of it.

Elliott was favoured to win it that year. All the other cyclists knew that he was the best man and would win; but Elliott's own team-mate, a Frenchman named Jean Stablinski, pulled a fast one and beat him at the finish. That might have been unheard of in national teams but in race teams it would happen from time to time, even though he should have slowed down to let Elliott win that race and the championship.

As I said, Elliott actually once wore the yellow jersey in the Tour de France, but he didn't have a strong enough team behind him, and it was the time when you had the likes of Jacques Anquetil, who was one of the greatest time-triallists ever. Anquetil is not long dead. I met him as a journalist when I was covering the Tour. He was an unbelievable time-triallist.

Elliott didn't talk too much about not winning the Tour de France. After retiring he had a sad old life in the end. He had invested in property in France, which he was robbed of by someone—the usual story of getting involved in a business you know nothing about. Two weeks after his father's death Shay tragically took his own life in 1971, when he was only thirty-six years old.

There have been a lot of good Irish cyclists, not necessarily in the same league as Elliott, Roche and Kelly, but one who immediately jumps to mind is Peter Crinnion, another Bray man who rode in the Tour. To even get into the Tour is an achievement. Stephen Roche's brother Laurence and his son and nephew have all ridden the Tour, so you could say the Roche family are ahead of everybody.

Peter Doyle was a great cyclist. He never rode the Tour de France but he won the Tour of Ireland a few times.

One up-and-coming Irish cyclist to keep a close eye on is Dan Martin, who made history in April 2012 by becoming the first Irishman in decades to win a classic when he beat the favourite, Joaquim Rodríguez, at the last of the Ardennes Classic in Belgium. It was Ireland's third win in this race, following Seán Kelly's victories there back in 1984 and 1989.

Martin is the son of Stephen Roche's sister, Maria, and the former British champion Neil Martin. He was the first Irishman to win a world tour stage race in the Tour of Poland in 2011. The latest rankings had him at number 8 among the world's best riders.

Speaking of keeping it in the family, Nicolas Roche is another great Irish rider. But he will never eclipse his father's record of winning the Tour de France. I think it is impossible to follow your father unless you are better than him. And the ironic thing here is that nobody actually wants you to be better than him, because he is an icon, and if you become another icon then they have to make up their minds, 'Is the son better than the father?' In the Walter Mitty way we go on about sport, who is better, Messi or Ronaldo, or, for that matter, Bing Crosby or Frank Sinatra? Who knows who is better than whom? That's what keeps sports going, fellas at it all the time about who's the best hurler of all time. 'Ah, Henry Shefflin.' Only to be met with an adamant difference of opinion from friends who'll retort, 'No, I don't agree with you.' And that's what keeps it going. Now if something else comes into it—a third factor, such as drugs—well, then it's not a level playing-field any more.

Apart from being an excellent rider, Nicolas is also a total gentleman. I attended a sports event in Áras an Uachtaráin for sports stars who were 'Champions of the World'. There was a long queue to meet and greet President Mary McAleese. I was standing beside her, identifying each person to her as they came along. Young Nicolas Roche came in, well dressed, with not a hair out of place on his head, looking every inch a star. He met the President, the same as everybody else, but he did stand out. When he was gone President McAleese turned to me and said, 'That boy Roche is very impressive, isn't he? He looks well, acts well, and speaks well.' I replied, 'Sure he couldn't but be when you look at his father.'

While the Tour de France gets more media exposure, I have to say the Giro d'Italia is its equal in every way, and the Vuelta a España wouldn't be far behind in my opinion. The Spanish tour is almost equally good, though it was later starting so it doesn't hold the same prestige.

These are the three great tours. The French event is seen as number 1 largely because of tradition and because it was first born but also because without fail it gets all the top teams. The Italians are trying hard and, in fairness, theirs is just as good. The Italian tour stands out for me because of the difficulty of the climbs and of course the fabulous weather. I think Italy is one of the most beautiful countries in the world.

It is nearly impossible for one man to win the two Tours, because you have to throw all your eggs into the one basket, but Roche won three. As I pointed out earlier, he became only the second cyclist in the history of the sport, together with the legendary Eddy Merckx, to win the so-called Triple Crown of Cycling in 1987 by winning the Tour de France, the Giro d'Italia and the Road World Championship in one calendar year.

But the Italian fans became livid when Stephen took the leader's pink jersey from his Italian team-mate to win the Giro; the hostility towards him was so frighteningly over the top that he was attacked by fans on the finishing line and even had to take the precautionary measure of having a special cook look after his dietary needs while he was there to make sure he wasn't poisoned, as well as having his bike under 24-hour surveillance so it wasn't tampered with.

'That was very scary. The Italian public got very aggressive. People were standing around for hours waiting, so when I got there they were half-drunk and they had rice and wine in their mouths and as I was going by they'd spit it at me. It was terrible. They had banners, "Roche, go home!" The crowd jumped over the barriers and they were hitting me. I reacted like, "Do what you want, but I'm not going home."'

Stephen Roche and his friend Seán Kelly were the last two cyclists to put Ireland on the international stage. Kelly won the Tour of Spain, so between them the two Irish kings won the three big ones.

Kelly was one of the greatest riders ever, even though he never won the Tour de France. At one point in the mid to late 1980s Roche and Kelly between them won every important race in the world: one-day classics, mini-tours, grand tours; between them they won everything. It was amazing.

Neither was better than the other. Roche was outstanding, as winning the Giro d'Italia and the Tour de France would suggest. He was a supreme all-rounder. There are difficult sections in cycling: there is sprinting, there is climbing and there is flat racing and time-trialling. But no-one expected him to win the Italian tour.

The best sprinter, without a doubt, is Kelly; in fact he was *de facto* world champion for seven or eight years. Kelly won the Spanish Tour. Cycling is broken up into what they call the grand tours and the one-day classics (Milan, San Remo, Paris–Roubaix, and Tour of Flanders and Liège–Bastogne–Liège), and in these Kelly was almost unbeatable.

Kelly's only downfall—if you can call it that—is the fact that he wasn't a climber, and you had to be a climber to win the Tour de France or Giro d'Italia. On the other hand, Roche was a magnificent climber. He was built for climbing. Roche's son is a different build and racer from his father. I would like to see Nicolas winning something big. It would be fantastic, because no father and son have ever done it.

I couldn't say who is better, Kelly or Roche. Kelly as a sprinter and a one-day classic rider was brilliant. Kelly would probably beat Roche any day in a sprint; but Roche would beat Kelly any day in the climbs, so we don't know who is better and we will never know.

But we have failed to produce riders of such a *different class* since those halcyon days for Ireland. Putting it bluntly, Stephen Roche lays the blame firmly at the Irish Federation for falling asleep at the wheel. It's hard to argue against him. He explains: 'Everyone was asleep during our careers, and when they all woke up and we retired there was a big hole there. You'd have to ask yourself if there had been more funding and structure in the Federation how many more cyclists could we have on the Continent today. Obviously there is something in the Irish soil that breeds athletes, no matter what sport they're in. I think if cycling got a better infrastructure it could produce a lot more good cyclists.'

———

While we have done well with these tours, it's surprising that Ireland doesn't have any stand-out cycling moments at any of the Olympics. There has always been a row here with the cycling people, because there have been different associations. The Northern Ireland group sent a team to the Munich Olympic Games to protest. They protested by hiding in ditches on the route in 1972 and jumping out into the race and joining it. Of course they didn't get away with it. I don't even know who they were, but they were apparently representing Ireland. They were protesting that a real Irish team wasn't allowed in it: if you were from the North you were in a different association from the one you would be in if you were from the South. We are in an unusual situation: you can compete for Great Britain or you can compete for Ireland if you are born in Northern Ireland, but you can't compete for Northern Ireland.

———

I think it's a disgrace that the World Track Cycling Championship doesn't get more exposure. It began as an outdoor sport but moved indoors, for two reasons: firstly, you could ride in bad weather, and secondly, they could charge people to watch it. The variety of events sustained over the whole tournament makes it one of my favourite sports. There aren't really any major Irish cyclists in it, even though an Irish guy named Irvine won a gold medal at the recent world championships.

The best countries have been the French, then the Germans, followed by the Italians; and in very recent times undoubtedly Britain had brilliant teams, headed by Chris Hoy, who has won more gold medals at the Olympic Games than Steven Redgrave did. He is just a *different class*.

The velodromes generally hold six or seven thousand people, so there is always a great atmosphere there. The bank curls at its steepest to 44 degrees, so crashes are nearly inevitable. They might wear very sophisticated aerodynamic helmets, but don't forget there are no brakes on these bikes! No gears, no brakes. This means you create your own speed and tempo, and you brake yourself by decreasing your pedal speed.

There are events like the pursuit, which is self-explanatory: one guy or one team starts on each side of the track, and at the start they chase each other and if you are caught you are out, but generally you beat the fella by being at your finishing line first. There's no head start and you begin at the same time.

The Olympic sprint has to be seen to be believed. Three men on each team; the first fella leads off and spins away; the second man takes over in a head-to-head with the other team's second man, and he then spins away, and on the track there are just two men. With the last man there is one against one, and by now they have some speed built up, so they have to have endurance, power and fantastic speed. In the sprint, the sprinters would do 20 metres per second at top speed. It's a sight to behold.

The atmosphere of it reminds me of *keirin,* which is a race invented by the Japanese solely for gambling reasons. It takes place in an arena. People pay in, with children, and dogs barking, and you have your fancy and you bet on your fancy. There are probably six riders, who set off behind a motorbike; they draw for positions and they follow the motorbike, and he increases the speed and with about 700 metres to go he pulls off, and by now they are doing 50 km per hour. There is some finish then, some fantastic racing.

The World Track Cycling Championship is also an Olympic sport, but there isn't that much of it on television, which is a pity, because it is so good. I know there wouldn't be a big audience, but it could be done with the right promotion.

I have gone to the last four or five world championships, not to do commentary but rather just for myself as an ordinary spectator. I have been in the mechanics' area, and you could lift the bikes with your little finger, 7 kilos with everything on it—but then there is nothing on it. It's amazing. As a sport it's certainly a *different class.*

Chapter 14 ～

IN PURSUIT OF LANCE ARMSTRONG

Getting back to the Tour de France: I absolutely love it, but I have to acknowledge that it has been somewhat damaged by the recent findings about the American cyclist Lance Armstrong. Did you ever ask yourself why the pursuit of Armstrong was such an unrelenting chase? Why didn't the powers that be and the media go after other riders so vigorously? Look at Bjarne Riis, Marco Pantani, Alberto Contador and Jan Ullrich—each of whom won the Tour de France with a suspect prescription bag. Perhaps it is that Armstrong, with his unsmiling countenance and tough exterior, built up a personality wall beyond which visitors asking questions were unwelcome. Such an approach probably fed as many enemies as did his lies about several illegal substances.

If he wasn't a self-confessed drug cheat it would be hard to argue against naming Lance Armstrong as the greatest cyclist in the modern era. But sadly that's not the case. He would have been right up there with Merckx, in my estimation, if he hadn't cheated.

It's amazing that he got away with it for so long, but I suppose not every rider is going to be gullible enough to be caught red-handed, like Michel Pollentier, who was found with bags of urine on his person. When he went for a urine sample after the race he was able to push the button on this contraption he had purposely built and give them a clean sample. Unfortunately, it was a female sample! You couldn't make this stuff up. How could anybody think they'd get away with such a farcical ploy?

Drugs, whether they are performance-enhancing or habit-forming, are a scourge on society, mentally and physically demanding on the person. We are not sure yet—it's too early to say—what damage illegal substances have done and are doing.

Some East German women athletes in particular looked like they had stubble and beards and shoulders like front-row rugby forwards. I'm not sure how many are in ill health these days, but certainly it is very noticeable that they were pumping themselves full of steroids.

Some athletes have even died, such as Marco Pantani, the 'Pirate', who won the Tour de France in 1998, the year the great race began in Dublin. And then there was the American athlete Florence Griffith Joyner, who was dubbed the fastest woman alive before her tragic death in 1988. She died of an epileptic seizure, and even though the autopsy report categorically states that she didn't die from drugs, most people suspected that her death was drug-related. Even her competitors publicly stated that there was no way the incomparable Flo-Jo could have become sprint champion without drugs in Seoul in 1988. Before the Olympics she had run with a fantastic time of 10.49 for 100 metres, a result that at the time was far beyond the compass of most men. It is still a world record at the time of writing.

Perhaps the best, or most inventive, fiddle in the Olympic Games was by the Soviet army Major Boris Onishchenko, who was caught red-handed cheating in fencing. He had wired his sword with a hidden push-button with a circuit on it that allowed him to register a hit when required. He had got away with it in the world championship, but he was caught in the Olympics. He jumped in to have a hit and missed the guy completely, but it still registered a hit! So they immediately knew there was something wrong, and he was booted out of the Olympic Village. He was never seen again outside the USSR.

Then there's the infamous Canadian sprinter Ben Johnson, of course. I was in Indianapolis in 1987 for the world indoor athletics championship, which was the first indoor championship ever. Ireland had a small team of four that year, but we still managed to win three medals—a silver and two gold.

Ben Johnson was in the 60 metres and he was just a sensation. In his heat he was so fast off the blocks that they recalled the race because

they thought he had jumped the gun. He was like a bullet. People said,
'Nobody can go that fast!' Then they checked back and found that his
reaction time coincided with the gun, not even 0.00001 second difference between the gun going off and the start. It was just one of these
magic things.

Ben, as many people know, was a scapegoat in 1987 at the world
championships, where he won the 100 metres, and again in 1988. I say
'scapegoat' because he didn't test positive at the time. Yet if you look up
the record books you won't find either of those dates for his victories,
because although he finished first he was disqualified after the race. In
fact a long, long time after the race they found he had taken illegal
substances, and so his name and his records were wiped from the
books. There were suspicions about him—but everyone is always a
suspect—and it wasn't until after the Olympic Games that he had to do
a test. All the winners had to do a test, and they found he had something
in his system. He was disqualified, and they took the medal off him.

Johnson wasn't the only one in the race who was found to have
taken something. His coach, Charlie Francis, later wrote a book in
which he said that practically everybody was taking anabolic steroids,
but they only made an example of Ben. I would say that does no
damage to the Games, but other people would disagree with me and
say it has to have done considerable damage.

All the other runners in the race were moved up one place, but in
subsequent years at least half of those in the final were found guilty.
Poor old Ben was the scapegoat because they had to get someone, and
they got him, the biggest scalp.

All this sort of stuff went on for a long time. I remember being in
the media canteen in Seoul when an American friend of mine said,
'There's going to be two big stories in these Olympics. There will be
one story on a male and the other a female. They will be shocking.' I
automatically took it that the male was Ben Johnson; so later on I said
to myself, he had been right about that. The female was Flo-Jo. She was
sensational but, alas, she paid the price, it appears, with her life.

Illegal substances in sport are no new phenomenon discovered in recent years. Almost every Olympics has given cause for concern, except notably for those of 1896. Track and field athletes like the afore-mentioned Ben Johnson, fencers, equestrians, swimmers, cyclists have all been admonished over the years.

There was a woman called Danuta Rosani from Poland, a discus-thrower, who in 1968 became the first track and field athlete to be disqualified for drug-taking.

There was also proof that an eighteen-year-old German called Heinrich Ratjen competed in 1936 as a woman but was proved later to be male. (He only finished fourth anyway.) Then there was the most astonishing story of them all, involving the Polish-American athlete known as Stella Walsh, born Stanisława Walasiewicz, who represented the United States. She had the facial features of a man. When she won a gold medal there were no sex tests but she had to withstand all sorts of jeers and sneers. Despite the hostility she won her medal, and won it fair and square. Many years later in a shopping centre in Cleveland, when she had long since retired, while getting into her car she was caught in the crossfire of a raid by a criminal gang and she was taken to hospital, where she died from her injuries. It was in the hospital that it was discovered that she did indeed have male genitalia. It seems that she had a sex-change operation.

———

Getting back to the Tour de France, there have been too many drug controversies to count at this stage, but then you can't believe every-thing you hear. An example that stands out for me is Gert-Jan Theunisse, a Dutch cyclist, who had at least one great Tour de France in the 1980s. His power was awesome, and with his long, flowing locks and bulging muscles he looked special too—so much so that there were whispers on the tour: 'What's he on?'

In the middle of all this guff, and while broadcasting for RTE, I told Gert-Jan of the gossip doing the rounds. We were doing a live television interview, in which he adamantly denied taking anything and swore he was innocent. He was so determined to clear his name of all this that there and then, on the side of the road at the finishing line, he offered to provide a urine sample. He opened his shorts and was about to produce a sample when my producer stepped up and said that this wouldn't be allowed on television back home. And Theunisse understood; but we would have had one big audience for that!

I always felt sorry for the poor divil; he was so annoyed that he was caught up in this. I asked somebody high up about it and they conceded that maybe he wasn't on anything. He was never fond of any wrong-doing, but there was so much testosterone in his body that he had the look of someone taking illegal substances.

Wouldn't the innocence and beauty of sport be violated if some of the significant and magnificent athletes of our impressionable past were found to have taken something illegal? Lance Armstrong is an example; he not only ruined his own career but devastated sports fans. It was never meant to be this way. He showed great promise starting off in his career, and I now have to wonder if was taking stuff even back then.

It was in Oslo in 1993 that Armstrong became the world road race champion. It was a day of very heavy rain, leading to many accidents. Every time a wheel seemed to touch the white paint on the road there was the probability of a tumble. Armstrong was still in his teens at the time, but he won the event, and the Americans went crazy. I met Lance's mother that day. She was a stereotypical American mother, filled with enthusiasm and confidence about her son's cycling career. She was telling me, 'He is hoping to ride the Tour de France and even win it.'

At the end of the race—it was piddling rain out of the heavens—everyone was hanging around to watch this mighty fella. Seán Kelly and Stephen Roche rode that race and they all fell, I think. And even Armstrong fell, but he got up quickly. People were coming up to his mother to congratulate her more than Lance, and she didn't ride a bike at all! When they were all saying, 'He is one for the future,' she was replying, 'Yes, he has dedicated so much of his time and his life and his love to this. This is what he wants to do, and we hope some day he will win the Tour de France.'

I don't believe his mother that day even dreamt that he would go on to 'win' (for lack of a more appropriate word) the Tour de France an astonishing seven times. On that day you could see the potential in him. He didn't appear to be egotistical, but he was a driven man. Unfortunately he was driven to such an extent that he had to win at all costs.

In his very early twenties Armstrong was being spoken of as a star of the future. However, it didn't happen according to the script. He was found to have testicular cancer, and his career seemed virtually over as he battled the life-threatening illness. It was during this dark period in his life that we first witnessed his refusal to succumb, his resilience, and his sheer bloody-minded hardness. The drugs that aided his recovery from the cancer somewhat clouded one's impression of his state of mind and body. Almost before we knew it he was back on the bike and riding in the Tour de France again and was victorious in 1999, 'winning' seven consecutive Tours up to 2005. He won La Boucle and got a largely positive reaction when he won it.

But by the time he'd won the Tour de France in 2002 the whispers were becoming audible. People were constantly telling me, 'He's not clean. It's time he was out of it.' Thus began one of the longest hunts of a wrongdoer in the annals of sport. There appeared no way that Armstrong could escape, because he was tested with fervent regularity. Yet he kept eluding the chasers. At the time my attitude—which has since changed—was that any man who suffered testicular cancer has to be on some form of medicine, but I never thought he was cheating to the extent that he later confessed to.

Eventually the US Anti-Doping Agency and World Anti-Doping Agency and a small quota of zealous journalists cornered Armstrong. He resisted all attacks until the famous 'Oprah Winfrey Show', where, to a succession of yes-no questions, he admitted he had taken the drugs during his great seven victories of the Tour de France.

I wasn't very surprised when it came out, because David Walsh of the *Sunday Times* had been chasing him for a long time, and they got him in the end. He was adamant that he was clean, and they were equally adamant that he wasn't and were saying that he told lies, he told lies under oath. It was wrong then of him to sue the papers and journalists.

Sadly, those big wins have now been erased from the record books, and Lance Armstrong's name no longer carries the weight and importance it once did. His status on the bike is all but gone; he is done and done for.

Allegations were also made against Stephen Roche, and members of his team were found guilty, but the Irish icon has never been found guilty of anything. All his dope tests have been negative. His momentous victories were somewhat overshadowed when an Italian newspaper published a story in 2000 quoting Francesco Conconi, a scientist and sports doctor who had worked with Roche's Carrera team, stating that he had administered to cyclists on the team a performance-enhancing blood-doping drug called erythropoietin (EPO). In June 2004 an Italian judicial investigation published a report of their findings on the Carrera cycling team, which stated that a number of possible aliases for Roche, including Rocchi and Rocca, showed that he had been administered the drug in 1993. But nobody on the Carrera team could be prosecuted, because of the statute of limitations.

Stephen vehemently denies the allegation and says he finds it 'ridiculous' that he was being accused of taking EPO seven years after he had reached his peak, when he became world champion in 1987. 'Why wouldn't I be angry? Why should I say I was positive? I wasn't positive. I never failed a test. I was tested all the time. There's no evidence in there at all. I'm presumed guilty by association. I was part of a team; certain guys on the team were doing this blood-doping, and then because the doctors that were involved were under investigation . . .' he fumes, clearly still bitter about the cheating claims.

'How can you write such damaging things with no proof? All you have is a magistrate saying that. There was four or five code names in there, and they're associating them with Roche, but there's no [evidence], they're assuming once again.

'This thing was so big and so important, and I was supposed to be one of the guys involved in it, you would imagine that I would've been maybe contacted by the magistrate and asked about my opinion.

'These findings were in '92 or '93, I think it was, where it's nothing at all to do with '87. Why not go back and say, "Why is Stephen Roche still the youngest rider to win Paris–Nice? Is it not because he was naturally talented, maybe?" Why not give the natural talent a bit of credit in all this, you know?'

Never, in my opinion, has a truer word been spoken.

Now I am thinking how many other great cyclists, runners, tennis players, footballers are living in fear that somebody somewhere is trying to dig up old samples that would be taken out of cold storage, and the backside would be ripped out of the love for these maestros of sport.

My fear now is that they are following everybody, and the whole fabric of sport is in danger. I really do fear that. At the time of writing there is a big thing going on in Australia that would shatter the whole world of sport, particularly in Australian rules football and rugby league. Apparently they have proved beyond all doubt that a large proportion of Australian practitioners in sport have been on illegal substances for muscle bulk, speed, endurance—all that sort of stuff. It's mind-boggling.

There are probably Irish people who have got away with it, because there are so many other people in the world who are getting away with it, not just in sport, in everything. It's scary, really.

Chapter 15 ～

| IN A LEAGUE OF ITS OWN

I was about eleven years old when I saw my first League of Ireland match, in Oriel Park, between Dundalk and Cork United. That Dundalk team have a special place in my heart, because I thought they were great. I even dreamt that I was going to play for Dundalk when I grew up, and I was actually with them training for a couple of years, but my football career cruelly ended when I burst my knee, and that was the end of that. I was very sad about that at the time, but it doesn't worry me at all now.

There were some great players around then, including a man called Peter McParland from Newry who is the same age as myself. He played for Aston Villa and was a successful player in England and was on the Northern Ireland team that qualified for the 1958 World Cup in Sweden. McParland scored five goals in the final, making him the top scorer of his time. He really was a terrific player.

League of Ireland used to attract big crowds, but back then there was very little else to do, because television wasn't like it is now; there was no Sky Sports, no mobile phones, no nothing. So you followed your local team. Dundalk was my local team, and they got a lot of players, both from the North and locally.

One of the greatest occasions for Irish footballers was the European Cup final of 1968, when Manchester United had two local heroes at full-back, Shay Brennan, who later played for Waterford, and Tony Dunne, who played for Shelbourne before he went to Manchester United.

Shamrock Rovers then, as now, were the team to beat, and everybody loved beating them; they were the Irish equivalent of Manchester United in their day. They won six cups in a row, 1964–9. They hit a vein of form, and they had fantastic players who all came together at the right time. That team came out of the Paddy Coad era—a great coach and a great player. When he went, there was a little break, and then came this other great team that had Liam Tuohy, Frank O'Neill, Eddie Bailham, Jackie Mooney, Tommy Hamilton, Ronnie Nolan, Liam Hennessy, Tommy Farrell—who was an uncle of the Hollywood film actor Colin Farrell—John Keogh and Pat Courtney, who became sports editor of the *Irish Independent*. Now that was a great team.

In the last three years of that famous six-in-a-row era Mick Leech played in three of the finals and he scored five goals, having scored in each final. Now, he has to be one of the greatest strikers ever in the League of Ireland. He played eight times for Ireland.

To be bluntly honest, the Rovers team under Johnny Giles was not as good as the six-in-a-row side, but it was still a good team, because they had Giles himself, Dunphy, Ray Treacy and Paddy Mulligan. They also had my son Paul playing for them. Paul was a good player but he sadly got an injury at the wrong time. In his prime Birmingham City and Leeds United expressed an interest in Paul, but he wisely decided to stay in Ireland.

At one time there were three Paul McGees or Magees who played in the League of Ireland, and even to this day there are people who don't know the difference! There was Paul McGee of Sligo Rovers, who was excellent, and also played for Ireland and also for Finn Harps; then there was Paul McGee who played for Bohemians; and there was my son Paul Magee. And they were all in the League at the same time. Paul McGee from Sligo was perhaps the best of them.

Shelbourne, who always had a good team, had a tradition of playing, or trying to play, good football, and they had wonderful players like Jackie Hennessy, Eric Barber, Ben Hannigan, Ollie Conroy and Freddie Strahan, who once scored against England.

It seemed like Ben Hannigan used to go over to England practically every weekend, but obviously he couldn't afford that, but he would go as much as humanly possible to see Manchester United, who had Denis Law at the time. Denis had a habit of holding the cuff of his football shirt and making a motion with it, and Ben used to do that, and you would know he had been in England that weekend. The games in the League of Ireland would be on a Sunday, and he would be back in time after seeing Manchester United on the Saturday.

Bohemians were a good team too, with the likes of Jimmy Conway and Kevin Murray. Cork always had some very good sides too. Back in the old days they kept changing the name of the team: it went from Cork City to Cork United to Cork Celtic or Cork Alberts. It was basically the same team. There was one occasion in the Cup final when Evergreen United played against Cork Athletic in Dublin, which ended in a replay. There were two brothers playing, one on each side.

Irish teams have done well in Europe on occasion. Shamrock Rovers one time had a great away match against Bayern Munich, their great team that had Gerd Müller and Franz Beckenbauer. Rovers were leading on away goals and had the match finished with ten or fifteen minutes to go. They would have been through on away goals; and then Bayern got an away goal and won. That was one of the great performances.

Cork with Dave Barry in charge did fantastically well against Bayern Munich again and held them until the very end of the match, when the Germans scored a dramatic late goal.

UCD won the FAI Cup back in the early 1970s, and that put them into the European Cup Winners' Cup and they got Everton. They played Everton at Tolka Park and drew with them. It was amazing to think that they actually drew with Everton, a big team from England. Everyone thought the return leg at Goodison Park would be a disaster, and they held them to only one goal. So that has to be a top performance.

AC Milan famously came to play Athlone Town in 1975. The game was held at the old St Mel's Park, which was up this roadway that wasn't palatial, to say the least. You could imagine this great AC Milan team with Benetti and all these brilliant guys arriving in Athlone to play, and the look on their faces when they saw the pitch! But they couldn't beat Athlone, and they had to wait until the return game on their own ground to defeat them. They say it was the poor condition of the pitch, but any great player should be able to play on any pitch, in my opinion.

Of more recent times, the moment that stands out as the best performance by an Irish team has to be the game at Tranmere Rovers' ground between Rangers and Shelbourne, when they had to play it in Liverpool because of the inevitable crowd troubles. Shelbourne played great on that occasion. They really shook up Rangers.

When English football began to be shown on television, the League of Ireland teams began to bring over big names to get the crowds in. At the beginning of every season there was always a star-studded match or two; I remember Stanley Matthews playing, which was a huge attraction, because Stanley then, and even now in retrospect, was one of the greatest players of all time. A marvellous man, who played at top level until he was fifty.

Cork seemed to be front-runners when it came to bringing in the big guns. They brought in a guy called Raich Carter, an English international. He was one of these unique internationals who played for England before and after the Second World War. When he was forty Cork signed him, and he came over looking all silver-haired and older than his years, but he was still a mighty player despite the appearance. They brought over others also, players like Ian Callaghan of Liverpool fame; Geoff Hurst, who is the only man to score a hat trick in a World Cup final, played for Cork Celtic; Gordon Banks played for St Patrick's Athletic; and Bobby Charlton played for Waterford. My son Paul played against all three.

Jimmy Johnstone of the famous Celtic team, who won the European Cup in 1967 for the Lisbon Lions, played for Shelbourne. Jimmy Gauld played for Waterford and later got into trouble for match-fixing in England. Ironically, there wasn't one Irish player on the Celtic team that won the European Cup in 1967. The amazing thing about that Celtic side was that they were all born within an ass's roar of Celtic Park.

Bobby Tambling, who was an all-time top scorer at Chelsea, came to work and live in Cork, and for all I know he is still in Cork. He was a very good player and a nice man. His Chelsea scoring record of 202 lasted until May 2012, when Frank Lampard made it 203. The gentleman that he is, Frank rang up Bobby and even invited him over to London for one of the games.

George Best also played with Cork Celtic. I covered that match at Turners Cross, which is now Cork City grounds but at that time was the Cork Celtic grounds. They were all ready and dressed to come out when Best arrived by taxi with the officials; it was all arranged that he would dress in the hotel and come down with the officials, maybe to avoid getting into a mess with the crowd, or perhaps to make sure he didn't hit the bottle before the game. He arrived, and he played well; he didn't play fantastically, but he played well. But it was the end of his playing days, and he was really filling in time.

There have been some great moments in the League of Ireland, and a lot of them were with Cork. It's amazing the number of transactions that Cork have been involved in for bringing talent into the League of Ireland, but not to the detriment of their own home-grown talent. They have produced some great local talent as well: the O'Mahony brothers, Morley, Jacky and his son Pat, who is one of the leading goal-scorers of all time in Ireland. The leading goal-scorer is Brendan Bradley from Finn Harps, a Derry man and a wonderful striker, who got a couple of very good goals in the Cup final of 1974.

Also in recent years, just to prove that Irish football has something special, the number of guys who have gone from the League of Ireland to the top echelon of the game in England is quite remarkable. You take people like Kevin Doyle, who is a top Irish player, and Shane Long, both of whom played with Cork.

While I'm at it, Dave Barry, who was a great All-Ireland footballer and a Cork man, was also a star soccer manager for Cork. Dinny Allen captained Cork to win the All-Ireland in 1989, but he was also a star Irish soccer-player and played for Cork City and Cork Athletic.

I suppose Cork football will be best remembered for Roy Keane, who played with Cóbh Ramblers before he went to Nottingham Forest and then Manchester United. The next big thing after him from Cork was Stephen Ireland.

Waterford is another county that has produced some excellent players, such as Alfie Hale. Waterford have always been blessed with local talent, such as the Hales and the Fitzgeralds. The Hale brothers, George and Harry, at different times and sometimes all at the same time, had Alfie, brilliant Alfie, who played for Aston Villa, Doncaster Rovers and Ireland. There was a fourth Hale brother, called Dixie, who went to England to ply his trade.

Al Finucane of Limerick—what a player he was; one of the best! He went through his whole career without being booked. He might have seen a yellow card when he was forty-two, but by then he had played through his whole career, capped for Ireland several times; as good a player as you would ever get.

The Fitzgerald brothers were great too, with Jack, Denny, Ned, Tom, Peter and Paul all from Waterford, and every one of them played for Ireland at some level, either for the full team or the Olympic team.

Waterford was right up there in League of Ireland. At one time they brought over a couple of fellas from Coventry, and it says a lot for Waterford that these fellas came over in the 1960s and stayed and now live there. I'm talking about the likes of Johnny Matthews and Peter Thomas. Thomas was the best goalkeeper who ever played for Waterford and one of the best who ever played for Ireland—even though he was English and got to play under the residence rule. Johnny Matthews ended up being a referee in the Waterford League.

We mustn't forget that John O'Shea and the Hunt brothers are also from Waterford. In recent times other Irish players who have gone to the Premiership include the likes of Enda Stevens from Shamrock Rovers, who is now with Aston Villa. There is, of course, Wes Hoolahan, who played for Shelbourne before switching to Norwich City—and for the life of me I can't understand why up to very recently he wasn't one of the first names down for every international game. And he only got picked by 'Trap' for the qualifying match against the Faroe Islands in June 2013 because of injuries. There's been the likes of James McClean, who went from Derry City to Sunderland. Keith Fahey too has made a name for himself in English football.

Going back in time, Liam Whelan never played in the League of

Ireland, but his two brothers, John and Christy, both played for Drumcondra, which was a big team at the time. Tommy Hamilton from Shamrock Rovers went away and played with Manchester United. Jackie Hennessy went to Manchester United from Shelbourne.

Alan Kelly Senior played for Drumcondra and then went to Preston, where he spent his entire career, and there is a stand named after him. His son, also Alan Kelly, played for Ireland, and his other son, Gary, played for Ireland too, also in goal.

The two Alan Kellys as goalkeepers were replicated by the two Ronnie Whelans, both of whom played in the League of Ireland and for Ireland. Ronnie Senior played for St Patrick's Athletic and his son Ronnie played for Liverpool and before that for Home Farm.

Kevin Moran played one game in the League of Ireland; he was footballer of the year with Bohemians' reserve team and had one game with the first team. He played with Pegasus mostly and from there joined Manchester United.

Apart from Roy Keane, the biggest success to come out of the League of Ireland has to be Paul McGrath. It's nearly like leaving the best to last. My late son Paul was playing with St Patrick's Athletic at the time, and he came home one evening and he was telling me they had a great training session the night before and had a new fella with them on the team.

'You'd want to see him, Dad. This fella is going to be the bee's knees. You would think I'm exaggerating but he's just fantastic.'

I asked him who he was and he told me he was a fella called Paul McGrath. 'He can get up there and he can stay up there in the air, judging where to put the ball,' he told me.

I was pleasantly surprised when I discovered that Paul wasn't exaggerating. Here was a player who even Pelé once said was good enough to play for Brazil. McGrath was a fantastic player, and when he was in the League of Ireland he was a fearless player. He was able to do it when he went to Manchester United, and he was able to do it for Ireland also.

League of Ireland has never let us down, and the game of football is getting better—there's no doubt about the fact, the game is getting better. At the moment Sligo have a very good team and are League champions, while Derry City won the Cup. Derry have always produced great players, like Liam Coyle, who was one of the most artistic players ever; his father, Fay, was an international, and Liam was a beautiful player with a bad knee that was literally hanging on by a thread, but when he could play he was just fantastic.

Chapter 16 ～

THE BEST IRISH SOCCER PLAYERS

For such a small country it's amazing to think how many quality players we've produced down through the years. So here's my list of the best players to come out of the Emerald Isle.

1. JOHNNY GILES

Giles was without doubt the greatest player to don an Irish international jersey. I'm not the only one of this opinion: he was voted the greatest player of the past fifty years at the UEFA Jubilee Awards back in 2004.

Giles's overall reading of the game made him a *different class* as a player, as a manager, and now as a pundit. He knows the game inside out. He is like one of the great conductors: he knows all the scores and from the top of his head knows what parts of the orchestra to emphasise the point.

He could do everything himself on the pitch. Unusual in football, he was two-footed, which gave him a very important edge. He could see passes, and he could change the pace of the game. He was a key man in what was a great Leeds team. I remember Norman Hunter telling us, 'We always had three or four natural left-footed players on the team: myself, Terry Cooper, Eddie Gray. And we had three or four right-sided players, like Peter Lorimer and Billy Bremner, Paul Reaney. And then we had John, who could be whatever he wanted to be.' It just about says it all.

I had first heard all about Giles when he was still a schoolboy from his future wife's brother, Paul Dolan, who worked with me on 'Junior Sports Magazine'. Dolan, who was an Irish Olympian 400 and

200-metres sprinter, came into the studio and told me, 'You have to see this young guy playing. He's a genius.'

I went to see him play a couple of times. He was the smallest fella on the pitch, yet I knew immediately that I was watching a genius. So I knew Giles from the very beginning, before he made his name with Manchester United and Leeds United.

Giles is maybe the best analyst of the beautiful game that I have ever heard. He is a library of information. One time I was doing a match and he was joint commentator. We were chatting away about one particular footballer—I know I'm the Memory Man, but for the life of me I can't recall which player—and Giles tells me, 'He misses a good few chances with his head. Do you know why that is? Because he closes his eyes. He has it all set up and he goes to head the ball and closes his eyes, and if it's not spot on it misses the target.'

During the game this guy goes up to head the ball and it goes wide, and Giles says when we are looking at the replay, 'Look at him: when the ball is coming to him he closes his eyes.' Who else would notice something like that?

Giles was excellent as player-manager for Ireland. He played an attacking and pleasant-on-the-eye type of game, which is a different style of football from what we see these days. But Giles had good players, better than the ones toiling away for their country today. He had the likes of Mark Lawrenson, Liam Brady, David O'Leary, Paddy Mulligan, Steve Heighway, Don Givens and Frank Stapleton. He was very confident of his good players and very conscientious about them: if you were able to play and able to do what he wanted then you were on the pig's back. He liked them and they enjoyed playing for him, there's no doubt about that, which again seems to be a much different attitude from some of those playing under Trapattoni.

Giles's style of play was a style that developed in midfield, where he played himself. Giles's way was, if you have the ball, please don't give it away, because it's hard enough to get it. It's a team game played by individuals—which is stating the obvious; but if you have the ball then play it to a team-mate; if you can't play it forward then play it sideways, and if you can't play it sideways play it back. But whatever you do, play it somewhere to your own team. Keep the ball. If you do lose it, which no doubt you will from time to time, as the other team won't be fools either, then you immediately get stuck in to tackling and intervening and intercepting and work hard at getting it back again. When you get it back again don't be so surprised when it bobbles away from you.

On one side he had Liam Brady and on the other side he had Mick Martin, who was a workaholic, and that was a hell of a midfield, with Giles as the father figure in the middle.

I think he was unlucky not to qualify for the World Cup in 1978. The team beat France during the qualifying games and were only two points shy of qualifying. They should have made it, but we were done in Bulgaria. It was daylight robbery, and there is no doubt about that either.

Giles gave the Irish an impetus that they didn't have before, and the world finally began to sit up and take notice and realise that the Irish team were a good team. After a great spell at Shamrock Rovers (my son Paul was one of his players) Giles went on to manage the Vancouver Whitecaps and was awarded the accolade of North American Soccer Coach of the Year in 1982.

2. GEORGE BEST

People might be surprised that I have John Giles before George Best; and maybe I would be surprised myself if I read it in someone else's book! With the ball at his feet, Best was a *different class*. He was a genius, really. Like Giles, he could also use both feet and fought for his own ball. He wasn't a fantastic team player: he didn't have an overview of bringing other people into the game; but on the ball he was as skilful as Pelé or Maradona. He has done some incredible things.

I put it to you this way. Say we had saved up to go and see a game and he was going to be playing. Say we were walking up Matt Busby Way to go to Old Trafford and we met someone who says, 'Did you hear the news? George is injured and he's not playing tonight.' You would feel like going home, wouldn't you? How many players can you say that about?

As I say, George Best would have been up there with Pelé or Maradona, but—and there was always a 'but' with Best—unfortunately he never played in a World Cup, which wasn't his fault. How could he have played if the team wasn't good enough to play in it? He didn't get to test himself at a World Cup, so for me I'd have to say Pelé and Maradona are better because they both won World Cups. That's the only grounds on which I can't put him up there on an equal footing with those two. It's the same grounds as 'Who's the best tenor you have ever heard?' You could say Pavarotti or Domingo, and they have never played the Met in New York or La Scala in Milan, and that would have to cost them half a point. Of course there's also the point that Best would have been a much better player, particularly towards the end of his career, if he had stayed off the booze.

3. LIAM BRADY

Liam could do everything Giles did, except Giles could do it with both feet, while Brady could do it with his left foot. He is revered by Juventus fans, even though he only spent two seasons playing there. Perhaps it's because he scored the goal that clinched the title. He also played for Sampdoria, Inter Milan and Ascoli.

Just to prove how much the Italians adore him, I remember walking into the Stadio Olimpico with Brady as the 73,000 fans crowded into the magnificent venue during an Ireland game in Italia '90. We were walking up the ramp to the stadium, and these guys manning the gate suddenly saw Brady and began shouting his name and running over to him in turns to shake his hand. I told him that it showed what they thought of him there still, because he hadn't played in Italy in a while and hadn't ever played for a team in Rome!

4. PAUL McGRATH

I want to make the point that Paul McGrath, the Black Pearl of Inchicore, is not relegated to fourth place in a sense, because he is a defender-midfielder, so he wouldn't be on the goal trail like the rest of them. And because of that he is able to reach only number 4, for no other reason.

He is widely regarded as the greatest Irish defender ever to play in England. It was all due to his speed, strength and ability to read the game and make tackling look like an art form. Paul was nearly impeccable, a wonderful player. He was so skilful that he could play anywhere in the back four or in the middle, where he was placed in numerous internationals by Jack Charlton for Ireland. I will always remember being at Lansdowne Road and hearing the fans shout, 'Ooh, ah, Paul McGrath!'

He's probably the greatest player to never win a League title in England. Pelé once said McGrath was good enough to play for Brazil. What a compliment! I have no doubt that Pelé was right and that McGrath would have made the Brazilian team as a defensive midfielder or a defender. As Ron Atkinson said one day to me when an intoxicated McGrath turned up to play a match, 'If he can get the shirt on he can play!' But Atkinson thought so much of him that he was willing to let him go out and play. Amazingly, the boozing didn't seem to impair his performances on the pitch. He was even awarded Man of the Match!

He is also a total gentleman, as well as a dear friend. When my memoir, *Memory Man*, was published in the autumn of 2012 I was in Eason's in O'Connell Street in Dublin doing a book signing, and there was a big crowd there with a long queue, and somebody from my publisher, Gill & Macmillan, said to me, 'There is someone who wants to speak to you.' I was wondering who it was, and out from behind a screen appeared Paul. I said to the crowd, 'Everybody, you know who this is!'

So people who were in the front of the queue got him also to sign the book, which was nice for them.

Paul had told me, 'I'm very sorry but I couldn't make it to your book launch.' He had learnt that I was signing books and phoned the bookshop to ask how long more I would be there, and he was told about another hour and a half, so he decided to jump into his car and drove from Wexford to try and catch me to explain why he couldn't make it. Who else would bother their heads to do that? We had a great chat, and he wished me luck with the book and thanked me for the friendship and being helpful to him.

5. PAT JENNINGS

The Northern Ireland goalkeeper was one of the best in the world ever, not just Ireland. He had massive hands, which is a great asset for a goalkeeper. He had a great long-kick ability, so much so that he once scored from his own box in a Charity Shield final for Spurs. He was one of those goalkeepers who perfected the body saves: he could save with his feet and even with his back! He was just a *different class*.

He helped Spurs win the FA Cup, League Cup and UEFA Cup. He also won the FA Cup with Arsenal. But unfortunately, like Paul McGrath, he never won the League.

He is a lovely man. He played for me in the Jimmy Magee All-Stars GAA team. However, he didn't get his game in goal but rather in centrefield. He and the All-Ireland medal-winner Paddy Cullen— another goalkeeper, believe it or not—were the midfielders, because we had a goalkeeper, a man called George Hunter, who is a musician.

We had great fun winding up George. The boys would be in the dressing-room putting it up to George, our regular goalkeeper. They'd be telling him, 'You're in trouble tonight, George. Not alone have you one piece of opposition but two—Cullen and Pat Jennings are here!'

I announced the team as usual in the dressing-room and decided not to start with goal, as is the norm, as I would embarrass somebody, so I read the team from right full-back to left half-back. I said I would leave out the midfield for the moment, for reasons that would become obvious. 'Now,' I said, 'I have three positions left.'

I could see George was in a state, because it was the first week in years that he didn't have the number 1 jersey on him. 'Don't worry, George,' I said, 'because Paddy Cullen and Pat Jennings are going to play midfield, and you're the goalkeeper, George!'

George joked that I was probably the only coach not to pick Jennings in goal. But Jennings actually played sometimes as a full-back too in Gaelic football when he was growing up.

6. ROY KEANE

When Johnny Giles was once asked to compare himself as a player with Roy Keane he responded that he felt he was slightly better on the ball, and Keane was better at tackling. He might not have been aesthetic on the ball, but Roy was a powerhouse: he could do everything and had inexhaustible energy and an immeasurable will to win. He was a great player who could equally attack and defend.

The world is full of stats these days, even down to how many sneezes we do in a day! But I saw one recently regarding the number of passes made in a season, and top of that pile was, of course, Roy Keane.

I said it to him at the time. 'I see you are top of the league for passes.'

'Don't mind that,' he told me. 'Sure you could make that number of passes if you hit them the same distance—three yards, four yards. Sure anyone could do that. They're not the real passes!'

I said they were very important for the link, and he replied, 'Yes, the link is the important one.'

That's what Roy was: the link.

Unfortunately, he has an inability to suffer fools gladly—and he isn't one himself, that's one thing certain—and could ignite with rage on occasion. His critics like to argue that he was too demanding. I don't believe you can be too demanding if you're leading by example. He once told me, 'I never asked anybody to do something I couldn't do myself.' He was extreme on himself. Roy believed in himself; he believed that whatever he did had to have merit. The proof of the pudding is in the incredible games he had, like when he practically single-handedly dragged Man United to the Champions' League final back in 1999 with a great performance against Juventus, or when he played Portugal off the park in Lansdowne Road.

What sums up Roy best is the 2-2 draw with the Dutch in Amsterdam when Ireland went up 2-0 and then the Dutch came back fighting and scored two goals. At the end of that match everyone was celebrating, and Roy walked off the pitch in what appeared to be a sulk and said we had nothing to celebrate. I believe he was right that day. That's the way Roy is: he wants perfection.

I was given an insight into this complex, enigmatic character when we met during the Euro 2012, which turned out to be a bloody nightmare for the Irish team, who have the dubious honour of being the worst team in that tournament, after being hammered in their three games.

As I was arriving at my hotel in Warsaw I was walking in the door to check in when I heard an Irish voice behind me say, 'How are you? Where have you been?'

And I turned around and there was Roy. We shook hands. 'Haven't seen you in ages,' I replied. 'Must have a chat.'

'I'd love that.'

I then asked him, 'What about now?'

He couldn't do it now as he was meeting people for dinner. I asked him if he was free for breakfast in the morning, and he was, and we agreed to meet. We spent a couple of hours together over breakfast, and it was lovely. There was no slagging of anybody, no contentious issues at all; instead we just spoke about games and how things were going for him. I didn't even ask him how he felt about leaving Saipan in 2002. I think he was wrong, but I didn't bother asking him. I have no doubt that he misses the game. He didn't say anything directly, but he did more or less say he was missing it. I was then taken aback when Keane admitted to me that sometimes he could be his own worst enemy.

'Ah, we can all be our own worst enemy at times . . . Just try to cool it down a bit,' I advised him.

He was telling me how he was doing punditry for ITV during the Euro 2012. 'I always give it everything I have.' He told me he has a burning drive to be good at whatever he sets his mind to. I have to say that he was very good on ITV during the Euros.

That morning over breakfast I said to him, 'Look, nearly everyone seeks perfection, but it's nearly impossible to attain. I would try it in my own way, but I'm not so sure I would ever reach it. So, I wouldn't be admonishing myself over it.'

'Ah, yeah, but you know,' he said, shrugging his shoulders. It would take some convincing to get him to be more laid back about everything.

I think Roy would be a great manager for Ireland. Why? Firstly, he wouldn't suffer fools, and secondly, he would have the team driven. Yes, he might drive them mad, but he would have them driven. He would know which players are Irish and which are not; you wouldn't have to be born here to qualify for the national team but you would have to be able to play like an Irishman. I think he could be the next manager; whether he should be or not is a whole other matter. There are many fellas that would make good managers; Martin O'Neill would make a good Irish manager, and I think he would want it if he was asked.

7. RONNIE WHELAN

Ronnie Whelan was a lovely player, and he was a key player in Liverpool when they were winning practically everything. And if you are good enough to be a key man in Liverpool you are certainly good enough for my book. He was a *different class* too.

I think it's fair to say that he scored one of Ireland's most spectacular-looking goals against the Soviet Union in Euro '88—even if it did go in off his shin. Unfortunately he picked up an injury before Italia '90, and Jack Charlton decided to give him only a run-out as a sub against the Netherlands. He didn't fare much better in USA '94, when he only came on as a sub again to play against Norway. Charlton recounted in his book that Whelan was very annoyed that he didn't get to play a bigger part in Ireland's brilliant run in Italy; but if you're not fully fit it's hard to argue with the manager for not picking you, particularly as we had many quality midfielders during that era.

Getting back to the positives here, Whelan is a living legend in Liverpool after racking up so many medals during his career there. In fact he was in the team the last time Liverpool actually won the old First Division. And there's not too many Irish players who won the treble, as Whelan did back in 1984 when he picked up winners' medals for the League title, the League Cup and the European Cup.

8. MARTIN O'NEILL

The third Northern Ireland man on my list is Martin O'Neill from Derry, who captained his team nearly fifty times. As a centre midfielder who knew how to score goals, O'Neill was a key man in Nottingham Forest. Under that eccentric manager Brian Clough, O'Neill won the League title and the League Cup. Sadly, he was dropped from the Forest's team in the 1979 European Cup victory, as he was recovering from an injury, but he was back in the thick of it to play in the following year's European Cup and win a medal.

Unfortunately his career was cut short because of an injury when he was still only thirty-two, but what a distinguished career he had! As with Ronnie Whelan, he's one of a select few Irishmen in the modern era to win a European medal or, for that matter, the old First Division or Premiership League.

It appears that O'Neill learnt a lot from Clough as a manager too, as he excelled when he took over Leicester City and then Celtic, who he brought to the brink of a historic victory in the UEFA Cup, only to lose out in the final 3-2 to Porto under the self-proclaimed Special One, José Mourinho. But even though he was unceremoniously dumped as manager of Sunderland back in April 2013, something tells me we have by no means heard the last of Martin O'Neill. I think most fans would like to see him appointed as the next Irish manager.

9. ROBBIE KEANE

Any man who scores a record-breaking number of goals at the international level in so few matches is world class. For that reason he is in my top ten, but it's hard to describe him as one of best strikers ever. The critics among us will quickly point out that he never lived up to the hype and couldn't become a regular in top teams, like Liverpool or Inter Milan. Yet he impressed at the likes of Spurs, Leeds United, Wolves, Celtic, Coventry and now Los Angeles. It's puzzling why he's had so many transfers, and you wonder if it was a case of him getting restless, or of the managers at all these clubs not having enough faith in him.

If he had stayed at one club in the Premiership he'd probably be high up the list of all-time goal-scorers, when you think about how he's got almost sixty goals for Ireland at the time this book was going to press, and the next-highest on our list is Niall Quinn, with 21 goals. Keane is at present the third top scorer at the international level to be still actively playing and will probably make the top ten of all-time scorers in the history of the game if he manages to nick a few more before retiring. Now look at England, whose top goal-scorer of all time is Bobby Charlton, with 49 goals.

10. MARK LAWRENSON

Mark Lawrenson was a *different class* when it comes to reading the game. He has a quick brain and could play expertly at centre-half, as assistant centre-half, or sweeper, as it's more generally known, and centre-midfield. He could play as either of the full-backs; he was just very, very good. In fact he played in all these positions for Ireland. Jack Charlton in his autobiography describes Lawrenson as one of the best players ever to don the Irish jersey. Charlton even argues that we could have won Euro '88 if he had a fit Lawrenson and Liam Brady in the team. Lawrenson won five title medals with Liverpool, but sadly his career was cut short at only thirty-two years of age by injury.

11. SHAY GIVEN

Ireland has been blessed with an abundance of quality goalkeepers, with the names Packie Bonner and Alan Kelly Senior and Junior immediately jumping to mind. But the one that surpasses these is Shay Given, who is probably the Republic of Ireland's greatest goalkeeper ever. He is one of only five players to surpass a hundred caps for Ireland (the others being Robbie Keane, Kevin Kilbane, Steve Staunton and Damien Duff).

At the international level Given kept fifty-five clean sheets, which is impressive. He certainly kept Irish hopes alive in many games, but his sharpness was clearly gone near the end in Euro 2012. I think he made the correct decision in retiring when he did. He and Packie

Bonner, our two finest keepers, have brought pride to Donegal.

At the club level Given is one of the best players ever to grace the Premiership and not win the League. I was surprised that Celtic sold him off before he ever got to play a League game in Scotland, but he quickly stood out at Blackburn and then later at Newcastle United. I'm all the more surprised that one of the big clubs didn't snap him up. At one point there was a lot of speculative talk about him going to Arsenal, and Trapattoni even said he'd recommended Given to some Italian clubs. For the life of me I can't think why it took Given until he was thirty-two years of age before Man City snapped him up, for a reported £7 million—and even City weren't a big club at that point, even though they had money to burn. He did win the FA Cup with City, but unfortunately the English goalkeeper Joe Hart emerged to replace Given as the team's permanent goalie, just as they were getting into their stride. It's a shame that he was forced out of the team and took a transfer to Aston Villa—and, by doing so, missed out on a League medal by only one season. But still, he was a *different class* during his prime.

Chapter 17 ↽

| THE NEED FOR SPEED

One of the favourite sports that I follow is Formula One racing. I've loved it ever since the first official world championship, which was held in 1950. Few sports can match Formula One for glamour and drama. The speed, of course, is alarming. You get a thrill from looking at the beautiful bodies (not all of them belonging to cars!).

I never covered Formula One as a commentator but I follow it and I try to see at least one grand prix a year. I have been to watch it at Monaco, Budapest, Monza, Catalonia, which is the Spanish grand prix held outside Barcelona, and the Silverstone in Britain. One of the most fascinating of them all is Spa-Francorchamps, which is an amazing place, because the weather changes so much there: from the top of the hill in Flanders in the trees it could be pouring rain, and then you come down into the valley and the sun is shining. That can give them trouble with tyres and how they are going to drive it.

The stand-out one from a 'buzz' point of view is Monaco, because the crowd is right on top of it and everybody comes to see it. When you look up from the start-finish straight they are dotted like ants on the hill, with people outside their houses watching it and these Lilliput-like figures in their cars dashing around the place.

The streets are too narrow for it really, and there are very few passing opportunities, but it is the glamour and the colour! It goes right under the Loews Hotel and comes out down by the water, and all the yachts of the super-rich are there, and then it comes out up the other side onto the hill, and above it is the Rainiers' palace, where Princess Grace Kelly once resided.

Monaco is a hard race to win, because, as I say, it is difficult to overtake as the roads are too narrow there. You need to get in front quick, but you can land yourself in trouble if you spend too long getting petrol and then end up behind. There have been changes over the years—notably the DRS (drag system) has been rejigged—but positions are now changing and are so scientific that when the car stops to change in the pit lanes it can also help them to gain a race position if their crew is quick enough off the mark. They are taking 6.1 seconds for putting on four wheels! These fellas are just incredible. Now one of the teams is hoping to get the pit stop down to 4 seconds, and if they do that they will beat a couple of stars.

I would reckon that the big star in Formula One for the next few years will be Lewis Hamilton, who went to Mercedes in 2013. (He is called Lewis after Carl Lewis, the famous Olympic athlete.) Lewis would be one of the top racers, and you would be expecting him to be world champion again now that he's with Mercedes.

At the moment the four best drivers in the world would be Sebastian Vettel, a German who has had three world championships in a row, Jensen Button, Lewis Hamilton, and Fernando Alonzo.

Over the history of the sport Michael Schumacher would be my top driver, because he was world champion seven times. It is incredible that you can be champion seven times. I also highly rate the first Frenchman to win the world title, the man they called the Professor, Alain Prost.

Unfortunately, Ireland hasn't produced any world-class racers. Yes, there was Eddie Irvine, but he was only ever runner-up and never fulfilled his potential. Our biggest success was Eddie Jordan, I suppose, but he was not a driver. There was Derek Daly from Dundrum, who drove in a grand prix, and John Watson from the North won a grand prix, but they weren't in that league.

Getting back to the big names, the late Ayrton Senna was exceptional. He was regarded by his contemporaries as the greatest racing driving of them all. I was at the Hungarian grand prix and I began asking any driver or engineer I met who the greatest driver was. I told them, 'I know who you are going to say, but I want to know why.' They all said basically the same thing: 'Because of Senna's attention to minute detail. If he can get a millimetre on a turn to maximise something he will get it.'

Senna was at a function that we were all invited to one night in a restaurant. He came in and everyone turned around and they all wanted pictures and autographs. This guy wanted to get a picture with Senna, and he agreed readily, and they asked me if I would take the picture. I'm not a photographer, but I said of course I would. I hold up the camera and ask what button I press, and Senna—who didn't know me from Adam, and didn't know the guy who had asked for the picture, knew nothing about us—said, 'Hold it a minute. The lens is not totally open.' The lens was partially closed, a twelfth of an inch, and it was semi-dark, and he noticed that. I said to myself, 'That is attention to detail, especially when it wasn't his camera, wasn't his picture, wasn't his friend; and yet he still noticed that detail.' I knew then that I had answered the question that I had been asking everyone.

Many fans and drivers would say that the Argentine Juan Manuel Fangio was the best there was behind the wheel of a Formula One car. He won the world championship five times and he had a record number of pole positions. I met him on the plane coming back from Argentina in 1977. The man dubbed 'el Maestro' and also 'el Chueco' (the bow-legged) did an interview with me on that plane journey, and I thought to myself, 'I'm talking to the fastest man in the world at the highest elevation I was ever at,' which was probably 33,000 feet. To this day he still has the highest winning percentage in Formula One—a remarkable feat when you consider how technology has dramatically improved since the days when he was behind the wheel.

Even the great Michael Schumacher once said, 'Fangio is on a level much higher than I see myself. What he did stands alone, and what we have achieved is also unique. I have such respect for what he achieved! You can't take a personality like Fangio and compare him with what has happened today. There is not even the slightest comparison.'

I might not have done commentary on Formula One racing, but I have been behind the wheel of one of these fabulous flashy cars. A few years ago I was watching television one night and I saw a race in the dark in Abu Dhabi, which was being conducted under floodlights. It was fascinating watching the cars in the dark on a track that runs between hotel buildings.

It was so fascinated that I said to myself, 'I'm going to go to it the next year.' The following year I was there, and it was really enjoyable. I actually went back again this year (not for the grand prix) while working on this book. I asked the concierge in the hotel one day, 'Could I get someone to drive me around the track? Was it allowed?' He told me it wasn't but that if I went down to gate 30 there is a racing school there that might be able to do something. And I asked them the same thing there. I was delighted when they agreed and asked me if I wanted to drive myself. Of course I said, 'No, thank you. I wanted to be driven around the track by a real driver.' So they got me the senior teacher, who himself is a pro driver of some substance, and they were going to give us an Aston Martin but said this car would be faster, a 6-litre Mercedes, which is the car they use in front of the race.

I get into the car and put on the fire mask, then the helmet, then the other fire mask, and then all the straps. And then after all this he said, 'If you are nervous at any time, just tap.' He took off screeching. The longest straight in Formula One is the straight in Abu Dhabi, and my God he let it out on that straight! I asked him what we were doing on the straight and he told me 269 km per hour (about 170 mph). It was something else! We did four laps around the track, and we even did the whole bit through the hotel where I was staying. It was brilliant.

I had already driven on my own (not at racing speed) in Monte Carlo, and I had been driven at Monza, but not at this enormous speed. I was also driven in the Spa-Francorchamps in Belgium, but never with such intensity as this. The driver said, 'Do you want me to drift?' And I said, 'You're in charge.' And, coming into the corner, he drifted the whole back of the car around. My head was shaking for about an hour afterwards. Now that was exciting! So from one year to another I went to see it, and then I went to drive around it, which is good!

———

I'm a fan of horse-racing. The big one at Cheltenham is the Gold Cup. It's the Olympics of national hunt racing in the Cotswolds every March, a festival that attracts billions in money, thousands in attendance and millions in television viewers. Someone once said that Ireland has never invaded anywhere, but that is not true, because every March we invade that part of England.

Ireland hits the scene in and around Prestbury Park, but not every Irish visitor around the time of Cheltenham is there for the hunt festival: not all of them go to the races. In fact you will meet many Irish people in the Stratford-upon-Avon area because they go there to play poker. There is a huge poker school there at the same time as Cheltenham, and these guys don't ever see a horse or a bookie. I met a white-faced man when I was heading out one morning and I asked him if he was going to the races and he said, 'Nah, I'm not going. I'm going to bed!'

I had a horse that ran in Cheltenham. I was part of a syndicate. My share was a quarter of it, with such fellas as Tim O'Connor (RTE), Seán Boyne (*Sunday World*) and Peter O'Neill. The horse was called Redundant Pal (not named after me); it ran well, but it didn't win. Because we owned it it meant we were able to go down into the unsaddling enclosure with the big boys, and that was thrilling.

I never backed our horse anyway, because my idea was that if it won it would make as much money as if I had backed it, and if it didn't win then I wouldn't be down money and it wouldn't make any difference!

The stand-out Cheltenham moment for me would be one I wish I had been around for, called the Golden Miller, but sadly that was before my time. I suppose the jockey who stands out for me—and I never met him—was Gordon Richards, who rode his way to a knighthood. I think he was the first jockey to be knighted (as far as I know the only jockey to be knighted). He won every race and he won them more than once and finally won the Derby in 1953 on a horse called Pinza. Horse-racing wasn't a big thing for me, but Gordon Richards was. He was the champion jockey every bloody year for a quarter of a century, and even children would be putting pennies on him in a race. I was only about nine when he was a champion jockey and I still have fond memories of him.

There were some great Irish horses in Cheltenham, like Prince Regent. Arkle, of course, was the greatest horse ever ridden over jumps. He was ridden by Pat Taaffe from Co. Meath. Arkle will be the one that everybody will always remember. It was the best, as far as Ireland was concerned. We have so many Irish winners and Irish jockeys, like Tony McCoy from Moneyglass, and Ruby Walsh, who was without doubt one of the greatest jockeys ever.

The two top horse-owners for me are J. P. McManus and Dermot Desmond. McManus is as sharp as a tack but a decent fella who has been a great patron of the turf. People say that Desmond is a perfectly decent bloke and pretty straight as financiers go, but he is not a sympathetic public figure, for some inexplicable reason, despite all his success with Celtic, as an Irish institution across the water.

Horse-racing is something we Irish excel at. If you were to name the top three things where Ireland either leads the world or is very close to the top of the league table you would have literature, music and horse-racing. Perhaps there are one or two other things, but those are the three that immediately stand out.

And if Cheltenham is the Olympics of national hunt racing, then Ireland is clearly top of the pile, with fourteen winners in 2013—one ahead of Britain—on thirteen winners. It's astonishing. In no other sport would we be so consistently successful. Look at how badly both our soccer and our rugby team have played in recent times, yet there are pages and pages and hour after hour of them on television.

———

I was lucky enough to see the baseball World Series in person in 1964 during a trip to New York. The Yankees had some great players, like Roger Maris and Mickey Mantle. They called Yankee Stadium the house that Babe built: Babe Ruth played there in the 1920s and 30s.

For those not familiar with the World Series, this annual championship is the best of seven play-off games, with the winning team being awarded the Commissioner's Trophy. It was begun as a competition between the winners of the American League (AL) and National League (NL). The first side to win it in 1903 was Boston (AL), later known as the Red Sox. It was boycotted the following year when the then manager of the New York Giants (who later moved to San Francisco), John McGraw, refused to allow his side to compete in the event because he claimed the AL was inferior!

The final I saw was between the NL champions, St Louis Cardinals, and the AL champions, New York Yankees. The Cardinals won the 1964 World Series with a score of 4-3, which was played out over eight days, thanks to their great pitcher Bob Gibson.

The Yankees were managed at the time by a man called Lawrence 'Yogi' Berra. A former Yankees player, he is in the record books as one of a handful of managers to lead teams from both the NL and AL to the World Series.

Yogi's language was quirky: he got everything mixed up, and he practically created a new version of the English language. One of his famous sayings was 'Nobody goes there any more, it's too crowded'! He also once said, 'I really didn't say anything I said.' He was one of the greatest players of the game ever and is in the Hall of Fame.

If you go to an American sports event, and particularly baseball, the place is always packed. But I reckon the crowd spend more time running to food stands and toilets than watching the event they came especially to see. I don't know how they have the time to follow the game at all, because they are constantly walking around with super-sized trays of hot dogs, cold dogs, burgers, fruit, ice cream, and beer. It's funny to observe. The organisers are forced to play music to get the fans' attention when something important is about to happen in the game. It is amazing how short the adult American attention span is; it seems to just pass them by.

Baseball is an American institution really and is in a *different class*— no doubt about it. It is full of stories that become wonders of the age. I suppose the big story—which is long before my time—is the 1919

World Series in which some of the Chicago White Sox allegedly sold out and threw the game. They call it the Black Sox.

People will tell you that American football is the most popular sport there, but traditionally it's baseball. The Yankee Stadium that I visited all the way back in 1964—and on many other occasions—has now been replaced by a new Yankee Stadium right beside it. What they do in America is implode buildings and then you go back the following week and there is a car park on the old site with a new stadium beside it. In Atlanta for the Olympic Games in 1996 there was a perfectly adequate stadium, the Atlantic Falcons' baseball team. Yes, it was an old stadium but it was perfectly functional, but that didn't stop them from knocking it down on the eve of the Olympics and making it into a car park for a new stadium beside it.

———

Basketball is also one of my favourite sports. In the 1992 Olympic Games I was there to do the commentary at the boxing games, but across the road from there the basketball was taking place, and it was an opportunity to see perhaps the greatest basketball team ever assembled, in the shape of the famous Dream Team of the USA, which included all the iconic figures, such as Magic Johnson, Patrick Ewing, Michael Jordan, Larry Bird, and the Mailman, Karl Malone.

That was a fantastic team; they won by an average of 43 points and averaged 117 points per game. Really it was only a case of handing them the medals! So famous were they—individually and collectively—that the first day they played against Angola, who had qualified out of the African continent, the Angolan team were looking for autographs and pictures before the game! I was there, and that was powerful to see.

Chapter 18 ∿

| GREAT RUGBY MOMENTS

The All-Blacks game against Munster is regarded as the biggest moment in Irish rugby history. Personally I think it was overrated. Yes, I'll concede it was a special game. Back then Munster weren't a club team: they were called a club for convenience, but it wasn't a club. I wasn't at the game, because I felt it was just another case of the All-Blacks on tour and they were meeting Munster, who nobody was giving a chance in Hell of winning. It sent shock waves around the rugby world when Munster won.

But—and there's always a 'but'—when a country is on tour they don't play their top team in a warm-up game, they play their midweek team, which is what would have been played that time, and is now conveniently forgotten. It is overrated because the All-Blacks on tour in midweek play their second strength, so to speak. Obviously if you are good enough to be on an All-Blacks tour you'd think there is no such thing as a second-strength team, but there is, and that's the team that played Munster. Nonetheless Munster beat them, and beat them well.

We have never beaten the All-Blacks, because we are simply not good enough, even though we have come close on occasion. But you would imagine that somewhere along the line we would have beaten them.

On the national level, the two big stand-out moments for Ireland were winning the Grand Slam twice, in 1948 and 2009. We lose matches we shouldn't lose, like Scotland in 2013. One thing that amazes me about the whole thing of rugby is that it has gathered a massive publicity wagon as it has gone along in recent years. Television has helped greatly for the popularity of rugby.

I have no problem with alcohol, such as Heineken sponsoring the European Cup in rugby. I would leave it be, because it doesn't affect me and it certainly doesn't make me want to drink. I don't think it makes anybody drink, but you are aware of it.

One of the things that fascinate me is the power of Munster rugby. I know Leinster have come along and won the Heineken Cup, but it was Munster who set this ball rolling. I cannot understand how or why Munster manage to work, because essentially Munster rugby is Cork and Limerick, who are not exactly bedfellows; they are not lovers. Cork and Limerick would have been a knuckleduster of a match over the years in any sport—Gaelic, hurling, anything—and suddenly they are together in this brand called 'Munster', which brings in thousands off the street. They are astonishing: it is one of the big success stories of publicity, there's no doubt about that.

Rugby is a natural game for the Irish. It's not a game of science, and you don't have to have wonderful ball skills to play it; you don't have to fiddle the ball on the top of your toe. The physicality of the game is what makes it so popular. As a nation we love physical games, and that's why Gaelic football is our national sport. The fans love it, watching the team just get out and get at it and run into fellas and knock them down. And it's a bonus when here and there you have a fella with fantastic skill who takes advantage of all this.

There was a great team in the 1940s, spearheaded by the wonderful Jack Kyle, who played at out-half. Older people of my generation, and perhaps even younger fans, would say that Kyle was the greatest rugby player ever to play for Ireland. He was one of the best—there is no doubt about that; but in my lifetime, which is almost nine decades now, the best player ever to play for Ireland is Brian O'Driscoll.

It is also very hard to compare a player in the professional era with players from the amateur era, because it's essentially two different games. Barry John said that the only two things that are the same in rugby now as when he played are the size of the pitch and the shape of the ball. Everything else is different.

So if Barry John, who is the best out-half that I ever saw, came along now he probably wouldn't get a start, as he was a little ghost of a fella at 10 stone. If the great Mike Gibson came along now he might not get a start. Eddie O'Sullivan was asked about this and he said, 'Only if he bulked up.'

The rules were different back in the good old days, and wing-forwards were different. Jack Kyle was sensational and he had a vision of a plan, and what's more he could play it; he took these heavy tackles, he was evasive and a great passer of the ball and a great quarter-back (even though there is no such thing in rugby, that's what he was) and he made the centres and made the wings.

It was a different game; it was a game where the forwards did all the bullocking, and Jack Kyle did all the football. You got scores like 3-0 or 6-3, whereas now you get scores like 29-21; you wouldn't get scores like that in the old days.

In some ways the game has improved, but in other ways it has deteriorated; it is much more like what Rugby League used to look like, because basically in the old game the forwards were always tight in their forward situation and it could be deadly dull. But when the ball came out into the backs there was room in midfield and it was basically sort of six against six across the field; whereas nowadays it can be twelve or thirteen against twelve or thirteen across the field and there is no room to move. It is just a different game. I saw Kyle play, and anybody who saw him in action said he was God.

Getting back to BOD, I'm glad he is going to play on for one more season. There was a lot of speculation that he might retire at the end of the Lions tour, but if anything the shabby way in which he was treated by being dropped from the squad for the last Test must have strengthened his resolve to continue. The greatest midfield player of his generation not just dropped from a team for the first time in his stellar career, but not even on the bench! You'd like to know what was at the back of all that.

Instead we can look forward to one more Six Nations season from the great man. Let's savour it, for it will be a long time before we see anyone half as good again. For my own part, I hope he scores the winning try in the Aviva to beat Warren Gatland's Wales out the gate. It would be the best possible response.

Losing out in the 2013 Six Nations wasn't his fault, and if he retired now he wouldn't be going out on a high: he would be going out stabbing and fighting. He has had a great and classy career.

O'Driscoll is just so far ahead of everybody else! He has everything: he has balance, work rate, great personal courage, great bursts of speed, and he gets into rucks that he shouldn't be in at all. He takes ferocious physical punishment that only heavyweight boxers should take, and there truly is no question about him being in a *different class*. He would get into any team that ever was; in fact it's a pity that one of the great nicknames in rugby history has already been taken. I met the man, who is an Australian Rugby Union player called John Eales—a big, big man, fantastic at everything, and he was also a kicker, wonderful in the line-out and wonderful in the loose. His nickname is 'Nobody'. I asked him why that is his nickname and the answer is because Nobody is perfect! And that would suit O'Driscoll.

Ronan O'Gara would be the best kicker of all time for Ireland; his record proves it. Ageism might have been at play for his not being picked recently for the team. Declan Kidney was successful with Munster, but despite winning the Grand Slam he faltered in the last few seasons and probably would have done better if he kept O'Gara on the pitch rather than benching him so much in the 2012 season.

It seems to me that what has happened with Kidney is that he had gone from a very cautious guy who doesn't act on impulse to suddenly making decisions on impulse. For example, O'Driscoll didn't have to be replaced as captain, and O'Gara didn't have to be chucked away like yesterday's newspaper. Declan Kidney thought it was time for O'Gara to go, but I don't like fellas when they are over thirty being cleared out for no reason. He is no worse or no better than he was ten years ago. It is almost as if he suddenly went against the grain of his personality, and that strikes me as what happens to somebody when they lose their own sense of purpose.

Sexton was the man in possession, and O'Gara was number 2. If he was going to dump O'Gara, the next lad in the race was Madigan of Leinster. They brought in this lad Jackson, while Madigan is a couple of years older and playing in a more successful side. To make his point, when he came on against Italy as a sub he made a visible difference, whereas I think Jackson was a boy sent on a man's errand, and it was desperately unfair to him. He is a good player, but I think his confidence is shot; his general game was very good in that first game he played where he missed the two shots.

Isn't it unfortunate that the media in general seem to say he is the kicker, because he wore the number 10 jersey? Who ever said that has to be the case? We are in a mentality now that the out-half must be the kicker, and poor old Jackson played well in his debut international but he couldn't kick. For example, Sexton is maybe a better all-round player than O'Gara, as he can defend his corridor.

Kidney is now gone. There was clearly a dissent in the camp in the 2013 Six Nations; they were not happy, and they didn't even look happy with each other. I'm sure they are trying their best.

But I don't think they were too happy when O'Driscoll was cleared of the captaincy.

If I was to pick the best manager of recent times I would say there wouldn't be much between Eddie O'Sullivan and Kidney. Sure being honest, it's all down to the players you have at your disposal. With an embarrassment of talent at our disposal in the last decade, perhaps one of the reasons we haven't done better is that we are not a dirty team. Look at the All-Blacks, who are one of the 'toughest' teams around. You only have to remember the time they flattened poor old Brian O'Driscoll. In New Zealand they say he blew a feather. Put it this way, if you did what was done to him to someone out on the street you would do time. O'Driscoll was speared into the ground that time on tour, no doubt about that, and it could have broken his neck or his back, or killed him.

New Zealand wanted to show him that they were the tough men of the world, who don't take prisoners. They were obviously not going to let some whippersnapper from Ireland show them how to play rugby.

There would have been people of Irish descent who played for New Zealand, but I don't think there has ever been anybody born in Ireland who played for the All-Blacks. I'm open to correction, but if there were there weren't very many of them.

These days in rugby it seems that to be good you have to be somewhat over the top with tackles, and the Irish aren't like that. Well, that might depend on who you are talking to, because, yes, we are rough players, but never dirty.

Years ago when we played we were taught to avoid contact and how to tackle, shoulders down and head tucked in. Nowadays they go looking for the physical contact; it's practically like American football, minus the helmets and padding. The All-Blacks are now the size that forwards were. Look at these huge fellas playing for Wales. Now, they are very good, but they are big enough to have played the second row ten years ago. The likes of guys 16½ stone playing and running like the wind, and we thought Jonah Lomu was good and fast!

When the subject of playing dirty comes up I always remember this funny story about Willie Duggan, who was a contemporary of Fergus Slattery's—no. 8 from Kilkenny and played for Blackrock, Ireland and the Lions. Willie could be dog-rough and unsubtle: he was the first man ever to be sent off in the Five Nations. One time after winning a game someone from RTE interviewed Willie and asked him what the game plan was. Willie, who wasn't the most cerebral of players, replied, 'We decided we would go out in the first half and kick the shite out of them, and we did so well that for the second half we would go out and kick the shite out of them again.'

Of course he was exaggerating. But what he said really seems to sum up the mentality of the game today. Today in rugby you just have big lumps of fellas running into each other, just looking for contact, rather than trying to avoid it. There are now some horrendous injuries in rugby. Take O'Driscoll, for instance. In the recent game against France in 2013, near the end he was at the sidelines and he had blood pouring out of him and was definitely concussed. Yet he went back on and played as well as anyone else.

After the Grand Slam there was a function that I attended where O'Driscoll got Sportsman of the Year (not surprising) and the MC had a quick chat and he said, 'It must have been a hell of a night last night at the dinner.' And Brian replied that he wasn't at the dinner. He said: 'I couldn't go. I went upstairs to change my clothes and I got vertigo and the whole place was spinning and it was worse when I lay down, and I just couldn't function, so I gave it a miss.'

I thought to myself, 'Is that normal for a young man, to get vertigo like that?'

His father, Frank, was at the dinner, and I went over to him and asked him, 'Is Brian not a bit young to have vertigo?'

'I wish you would tell him that!' he replied.

I was thinking to myself then, wasn't it something like that he had against France also?—where he was standing there and the whole place was spinning, and idiotically he went back on again. I think he will be talking to himself in twenty years. The hits are enormous, and the ones he gets he goes looking for them.

With Declan Kidney gone, perhaps the new manager, Joe Schmidt, will be able to bring out the best in the team. Hopefully some of the older players will continue on, but we have some promising youngsters coming up through the ranks now, like Donncha Ryan, who has appeared on the scene as a forward. Healy is a young lad who is a very good prop, and I think Madigan will make it big time; he could be the new Brian O'Driscoll. Tommy Bowe is very good. It's funny, we're very well off for backs at the moment, which we traditionally weren't before.

The British and Irish Lions is a massive tradition, and the biggest match ever for Ireland would be beating New Zealand, if we could beat the shite out of them somehow. You would need O'Driscoll at his powerful best, Paul O'Connell at his powerful best, O'Gara and all the all-time players at their best, and all four years younger! In other words, I wouldn't put my money on it happening any time soon.

I've named some of my favourite Irish players there, such as Brian O'Driscoll, Jack Kyle and Ronan O'Gara, but there are others on my all-time list. Paul O'Connell would have to be up there as one of our great forwards. With forwards you are talking about a different thing altogether. While nobody could beat O'Driscoll, Ollie Campbell and

Tony Ward were both great players: both had skill and brains. Karl Mullen, the hooker and captain of the 1948 team, was also a *different class*. Trevor Ringland has a fantastic international career too, even making the British and Irish Lions tour in 1983. Mike Gibson would easily be in my top five Irish players of all time. There would be little between Brian O'Driscoll and Mike Gibson: O'Driscoll would probably be the better forward and a fabulous leader. O'Driscoll loved being among the forwards, getting walloped. Perhaps one of his greatest moments was scoring three tries against France in Paris back in 1999. He had a lot of things going for him: firstly, natural balance; I would say if he wanted he would never be off his feet because of his balance. His pick-up was brilliant; he could pick a ball up off his toes as if knowing what to do and when to do it. He was also the master of the 'no-look pass', which Magic Johnson made famous in basketball.

Last, and by no means least, on my list of favourite Irish players is Tony O'Reilly. It's stating the obvious to describe him as a very good player. After he retired he once turned up in a limo to a game when there was a late withdrawal through injury for a match in Twickenham. Surprisingly, O'Reilly was recalled, because he was working in London at the time in Heinz and he gladly accepted, and and arrived out in a chauffeur-driven limo. He wouldn't have played great that day; he went through the motions really. He went down once in the ruck and Ireland are rooting away for the ball and someone in the crowd shouts, 'Sure kick his chauffeur while you're at it!' Whether it's true or not I don't know, but that has become an O'Reilly after-dinner story.

But during his peak O'Reilly was outstanding. People seem to forget that before he became a media mogul he was the leading scorer of his time. He still holds, in fact, the record for number of tries scored by a player for the Lions. He only played in two tours but he managed to score thirty-seven tries.

Brian O'Driscoll is the best we have ever produced, and he would have to be away up in the top ten world ranking. He would be a better footballer than Lomu, widely regarded as the first big superstar in the game. He was massive in every sense. But O'Driscoll is still a much better player, because he is an all-rounder: defence, can play like an extra forward, fearless, clever, a leader.

If you were picking an Irish centre partnership between 1965 and now, you don't even have to think about it twice: it would be Gibson at 12 and O'Driscoll at 13—no question.

O'Driscoll could have played for the All-Blacks. If he had gone to France I think he would have been talking to himself even sooner than he will be. French rugby can be violent. I suspect his father had a word in his ear about going to France.

But even if O'Driscoll does stay on for the next Six Nations, I don't give us a fighting chance of winning it. By the looks of this year it will be a long time before we win a Grand Slam again.

So here's my list of the world's best rugby players:

1. Brian O'Driscoll
2. Gareth Edwards
3. Seán Fitzpatrick
4. Jonah Lomu
5. Mike Gibson
6. Jack Kyle
7. Gerald Davies
8. J. P. R. Williams
9. Richie McCaw
10. Barry John

There was no way I could leave out Barry John. Some fella in Wales recently said in one of the papers, 'If Barry John ran through a field of corn the only people that would know which way he had gone was the corn. He could run through gaps that didn't seem to be there.'

He was truly fabulous—like all the aforementioned rugby players, who all deserve to be put in the *different class* category.

Chapter 19 ~

| THE FIGHTING IRISH

W illie Pep, who was an American featherweight boxer, was so outstanding that defensively he was always joking and ducking and weaving. It was nearly impossible to hit this guy. In fact it was said that he won a round in a fight where he never landed a blow—which could not have happened, but it has become true with the passage of time. It was because he was so evasive that his opponent couldn't hit him.

Pep, who had his first amateur fight back in 1937, is still held in such high regard today that he was voted number 1 featherweight of all time by the International Boxing Research Organization in 2005.

I believe nobody can lay a glove on the following Irish boxers. Rather than put together a separate list of my favourite amateur and professional Irish boxers, I have decided to mix them up in one list.

1. BARRY McGUIGAN

I don't think anybody would argue against having this featherweight champion in first place on my list. Barry won the world title in London in the QPR over Eusebio Pedroza, which was only the second time he had been beaten in more than thirty fights. When Barry McGuigan had you going you stayed going, that's certain. He was a great body-puncher, and he was a great boxing man. He loved it and knew it inside out. The tragic death of 'Young Ali' (Asymin Mustapha), who died after a fight with McGuigan, affected the Irish boxer for a while and maybe affects him still, but he went on with his job and went on with it well.

Unfortunately Barry defended his world title at Caesar's Palace in Las Vegas. In retrospect this was a mistake. He was a fantastic boxer, but unfortunately he lost the featherweight title in Las Vegas. There was something odd about that night. Firstly, the heat was horrendous: those who know these things say it was 125 degrees (52 Celsius), but other reports say it was 110 degrees (43 Celsius). I know that ballpoint pens were melting on the press table. It was ferocious. At the end of every round servants would come around and put wet towels on the back of reporters' necks.

Barry was in the ring with not just the arc lights for the television but also the sun shining down in the middle of a boiling afternoon. He told me he doesn't remember anything from the tenth round on, but by the end of the fight he was out on his feet. He was knocked down twice in the last round, and only for this he would have retained the title. I know this because I had befriended a woman who worked in the offices there, and I went to her after the fight and asked if I could look at the score cards. One judge had McGuigan behind, another had him ahead, and another had him level with the relatively unknown Texan boxer Stevie Cruz. McGuigan, as the champion, would have got the advantage when it was that close, which was the norm. Getting knocked down twice in that final round decided the one remaining judge, the one who mattered, to go for Cruz.

At the end of it all McGuigan passed out from dehydration, as he had no water from the tenth round on. But he was apparently shouting, 'Don't let them close my eyes!' because he was afraid of death.

2. KENNETH EGAN

In one way Michael Carruth would be better than Egan, because he won gold at the Olympics, but in another way he wouldn't, because of Egan's record of ten national seniors and thirteen consecutive finals. Just think of what you have to do to be in a final, to be trained to make the weight in one year; but to do it thirteen years in a row is remarkable, and to win ten of them . . . And in the middle of all that to win an Olympic silver medal. I know Egan feels he was robbed of the gold medal, but I felt at the time he was second-best on the day of the fight. Nevertheless I think I would have to give Egan my number 1 spot as an amateur, or number 2 on this list.

3. MICHAEL CARRUTH

I feel like admonishing myself for having an Olympic gold-medallist like Michael Carruth at number 3, but I'm sure Michael will understand. Any man who wins an Olympic gold medal is entitled to be number 1. It just doesn't help when his opposition is a man who is an Olympic silver-medallist and has all those championships that Egan has.

4. WAYNE McCULLOUGH

He first happened upon the scene in Ireland as a light flyweight, the lightest of all divisions; he eventually went up to fly and then bantam. It was in the latter division in Barcelona in 1992 that he won a silver medal at the Olympic Games. Unfortunately he got a bad eye injury in the semi-final against a Korean boxer. It bled profusely, but his eye wasn't cut. This was something that happened inside his jaw, and whenever he was punched on this spot it would make blood squirt out.

We were all wondering if he would be allowed to compete at all in the finals, but he passed the medical on the day of the finals and boxed out of his skin, as usual. He boxed a Cuban called Joel Casamayor, who is still around the pro ranks in America. He was a great fighter, who became world professional champion. I can tell you this: if McCullough had beaten him—and he wasn't that far away from it—he would have been given the Val Barker Award, which is best boxer in the Olympics.

McCullough was a great world champion. As a pro and an amateur he was a credit. I said of him once on the air that he was like one of those machines that you put a coin in and off he would go, boxing non-stop and throw eight hundred punches. Wayne was very special.

5. STEVE COLLINS

He beat Eubank, which sums it all up really. At some stage in his life he decided he was going to be the best pro he could possibly be. His life is certainly a rags-to-riches story, reminiscent of Rocky. After marrying his first wife in 1986, Steve quit his job as an electrician in the Guinness brewery to follow his boxing dream. He moved to Boston, because he wanted to train in the same gym as the reigning world champion, Marvelous Marvin Hagler. He won a good few fights in America and a title. He fought Mike McCallum, who was a great middleweight. He fought him for the title in Boston and he lost that fight.

After three failed attempts at a world title, Steve was thirty years old before finally achieving his dream of becoming the middleweight champion in 1994. He then relinquished his title without defending it, because, he says, he felt 'weak at that weight,' and so he piled on the pounds to fight at super-middleweight. It turned out to be a blessing in disguise. 'I came home to rest, and I got a phone call offering me the Chris Eubank fight at a heaver weight.'

Steve had only got the call for the WBO title fight at the last minute because Eubank's original opponent had pulled out because of an injury. It was Ray Close's fight, from Belfast, but he failed a medical for a fight that had been signed up, and Collins stepped in. He enlisted the help of the life-style 'guru' Tony Quinn in preparing for the match. Steve admits that he used the controversial figure in order to play mind games with the reigning champ.

'Chris is a very superstitious guy,' explains Steve. 'It was a mind game. He accepted defeat before defeat even happened.' It was a fantastic move. Don't forget Eubank was unbeaten when Collins got his hands on him.

Eubank didn't know what to do, because this whole Tony Quinn thing had definitely confused and spooked him. I think it might have been showman stuff, and it *was* showman stuff, wired to the moon. The other fella came in on a motorcycle; he didn't want to fight Collins in the end. He spent the whole night with Noel C. Duggan, owner of the Millstreet centre in Co. Cork, saying, 'I don't want to fight. I can't fight.'

Duggan told me himself that he had spent the night with this man, and he didn't want to box. Noel told him he would have to box, because the whole place was sold out, and asked him why he didn't want to fight. Eubank apparently said something like 'This man is on some sort of mentalist thing,' and he was afraid—not afraid physically for himself but afraid he might hurt Collins. That was his spin on it: because Collins was hallucinatory, or something like that.

Eubank, who once almost fatally injured a boxer, Michael Watson, pleaded with the promoters to pull the fight. On the night, Collins was a better fighter. The thing about Collins is, he has fantastic pride in his ability, and always had. Eubank might have been—I am loath to say this—technically superior, but technique is no good unless you have a fighting heart, and Collins had it in spades.

Not alone did he beat him once but he beat him again in the rematch in Páirc Uí Chaoimh in Cork, and with a bigger point margin. Steve used different tactics to win the rematch. 'I harassed him for twelve rounds. Before he knew what was going on the fight was over. I upset him; I didn't let him get into his rhythm.'

Collins won at two weights—he won at middle and super middle—but the first official middleweight champion of the world was an Irishman from Clane, Co. Kildare, called John Kelly, who was so good they called him Jack Dempsey, and he became known as the 'Nonpareil', i.e. the unequalled or unparalleled.

Collins was a bigger man than Eubank; he also beat Nigel Benn, the 'Dark Destroyer'. I think Benn was better than Eubank.

Collins, who is now forty-eight, is talking about coming out of retirement after almost fifteen years to slug it out with 44-year-old Roy Jones Junior, who holds the distinction of being the first pugilist in more than 106 years to win world titles in both the middleweight and the heavyweight division.

I don't want to insult Steve Collins, but I think Roy Jones would have beaten him back in their prime. There would have been a time in his career when Roy Jones would have beaten anybody, and he did. Jones was absolutely brilliant. I saw him at his peak as an amateur in the Olympic Games in Seoul, where he went to the final, and he was just brilliant against the Korean champ, yet he didn't get the decision. It was a massive robbery. I was doing the commentary and there was no doubt he won it, and then up came the decision, and anyone who wasn't Korean was booing.

In fairness to Jones I must say he was a good loser and didn't throw the head, which most fellas would have done. There had to be an inquiry into it, and when that happened they asked the Moroccan judge what happened. Two of the five judges went for the Korean, two for Jones, and one thought it was 50-50. The Moroccan judge said, 'I knew that Jones won'—this is on record!—'but in deference to our hosts I gave it to the Korean.' So Jones lost; and decisions can't be overturned. He then went pro, and he just went from good to very good to great. He simply couldn't lose.

Collins was always seeking to fight him; he even went into the ring one time to publicly challenge him. Collins is probably suggesting that Jones is afraid of him, but I have my doubts about that. I think it probably didn't make financial sense for Jones to fight Collins. You get to a stage where you can choose who you fight. It would have been a risk match for Jones, but not for Collins, and Collins would have given him a fight—there is no doubt about that: he had a great fighting heart. Remember that Collins put away Eubank, and he put away Benn. I'm telling you, Collins was very good and very disciplined, but I still think Jones would be hard to beat.

If the fight does go ahead it will depend on what sort of form Jones is in, because Collins has great pride in his conditioning and he would do anything not to let us down; he is that sort of a man. I don't know what condition Jones is in mentally himself; I think he might have enough of it now. Somehow I doubt the fight will happen.

6. BERNARD DUNNE

He has to be away up there. Bernard was able to do something that his daddy couldn't, but his daddy was able to do something that Bernard wasn't able to do: fight at the Olympics. Brendan Dunne Senior was the first light-flyweight Champion of Ireland in the 1970s. It was a new weight division; fly used to be the lightest. He even went to the Olympic Games in Montreal.

Some years later a young man called Bernard Dunne came on the scene. He looked really good, looked as if he was a cert for the Olympic

Games, but he was in reserve for the Games and he went to Sydney as a sub, if you will. If anyone had dropped out of the Olympics, Bernard would have been the next one in, which meant he had to be prepared, but he had no way of getting into the contest.

And I remember saying to myself, 'What a shame, because here was a young fella ready for the Olympics.' But because he wasn't accredited he couldn't get in to see the Irish boxer Michael Roche from Cork boxing. So we at RTE got him a ticket, and he came in and was joint commentator with me. As it turned out, he never did get to box in the Olympics, and so he missed out on something his dad did, but his dad missed out on something that he did: win a world professional title, which he did in 2009 at the O2 Arena in Dublin. The place was packed, and Bernard Dunne became a national hero. It was the same day that Ireland won the Triple Crown under Brian O'Driscoll.

Bernard Junior had charisma; that was the first thing he had, and whatever he had as a fighter he was able to maximise it by his control outside the ring, his ability to mix with the people and the media; so he was always going to get good press, because he was obliging. He was the same on radio and television, and he was very helpful to me in particular and to loads of other people.

He was just a terrific champion, with a smile on his face. Technically he was very good, and he had a very good agent and promoter in Brian Peters. Without him in his corner Bernard wouldn't have seen any of this sort of boxing in that particular time in Ireland. Brian Peters was outstandingly good.

7. MICK DOWLING

He won eight bantamweight titles in a row and two European medals. He would win regularly. What made him special is that he was an accurate puncher. The amateurs can sometimes be more accurate. It really is a different sport, because professional boxing is where you put fellas away.

8. CHARLIE NASH

He was a lightweight, he was a beautiful stylist and a terrific puncher, many times Irish champion and an Olympian, and he also had a good career as a professional.

9. PADDY BARNES

Paddy had to be on the list: seven times Irish light-flyweight champion sums it all up. He is the only Irish boxer to win two Olympic medals: bronze in Beijing in 2008; bronze in London in 2012.

———

Normally, most lists are round figures, but I couldn't decide who else should be nominated among all the other boxers in my estimation, including Jim McCourt, who was brilliant at the 1964 Olympic Games. Then other names that jump to mind include John Joe Nevin, silver medallist at the London Olympics, world rated number 1 bantam, twice medallist at the world championships, Michael Conlan, Fred Tiedt, Harry Perry and Charlie Nash. The only one I don't rate highly that is a celebrated name is Jack Doyle, because in my opinion he was just a showman. He never won any titles: the only thing he won was Movita from Marlon Brando!

He might not make my top Irish boxers list, but I feel one particular boxer deserves a special mention. The last man to fight Mike Tyson and beat him was an Irishman called Kevin McBride, from Clones, Co. Monaghan, just across the fields from where Barry McGuigan hails from. He was a giant of a man who was on the Irish Olympic team in Barcelona when Carruth won the gold medal and Wayne McCullough won the silver.

Kevin McBride, who was trained by Steve Collins's brother Paschal, was the super-heavyweight on that Irish Olympic team. He didn't win a medal but he went to America to try to make a few bob as a professional fighter. Kevin was a big, big hitter. Whoever was looking after him got him a bout with Tyson, and it turns out it was Tyson's last fight, because he was put down and beaten by McBride.

McBride should have cashed in on that, but he didn't. Tyson is some name to have in your CV; there's hardly a person in the world who doesn't know Mike Tyson, so imagine saying, 'I want you to meet the man to have beaten Mike Tyson in his last fight.' Tyson only lost six fights in his entire career.

———

It would be unfair to put Katie Taylor in my list of all-time great Irish boxers; she should be on a female-only list of our outstanding pugilists. But we only have the one, and therefore Katie Taylor deserves her own list.

It appeared to be her destiny to win an Olympic gold. Right from the moment she stepped into the ring and sparred with boys, Katie felt at home and soon had a strong belief that she was destined for boxing greatness. 'I'm going to go all the way to the top,' Katie told RTE when she was eleven years old.

She became a trail-blazer for women's boxing in Ireland when she participated in the first sanctioned female bout, held in the National Stadium on 31 October 2001. There have been many historical firsts in Katie's distinguished boxing career. She is the first woman to win five successive world titles and five European titles. It's been a long, hard, winding road, not just for Katie but for women's boxing in general, to win over the most ardent detractors.

Even the former world champion Barry McGuigan, who is now a vocal supporter of Katie and women's boxing in general, was steadfast against the idea of it until he saw the Irish champ in action. 'My personal considerations were blown away. Her skill, power, speed, technique and attitude are all top-class. Double left hooks, right hands over the top—it's just extraordinary.'

Billy Walsh, head coach for Team Ireland at London in 2012, believes sparring with men gave her an edge and contributed to her uniqueness in the women's game. 'She spars with men, beats men, fights like a man,' he told the *Irish Post*. The former world champ Lennox Lewis once observed: 'She fights like a geezer—and if a geezer was in the ring with her she would knock him out.'

In London in 2012 when Katie got into the ring for the quarter-final fight I was doing live commentary, and a thought ran across my mind: 'At this moment a nation is wishing her well, and she is the most talked-about person in the Irish team.' I was thinking, 'Everyone is with her. Everyone is for her, and they are all talking about her in pubs and clubs and homes, but nobody has ever really seen her fight before.' So I was saying to myself, 'Now she is stepping in, now there is pressure on her, because she is now going to show the people of Ireland that she really is as good as everybody says she is.'

The only other time Irish fans had seen Katie in action was during the night of the Hunky Dory fight in the O2, on the under card for the Bernard Dunne title fight. I did talk Katie up that night, and I told the audience that we were about to see a fighter who had the potential to make history. In my estimation she is Ireland's best contemporary sports star.

Getting back to London, Katie was brilliant; she really rose to the occasion. It was a tough fight, nothing in it, but she won it. I am lucky (and that is what it is) that I did 120 contests at the Olympics, meaning that I did nearly every fight that was on every day in London in 2012. There are no scores shown—I don't have a private monitor with scores or anything: I am looking at it the same as everyone else, and nobody is expecting miracles from me either. My head kind of knows who is going to win, or who has won, out of them all. Now this may sound boastful—and I don't mean it to be—but I was nearly right on every decision, probably more than 95 per cent. I don't know how I do it; I am not saying I am always right, though. The Katie final fight against the Russian was very, very close; I think it came down to two or three points. I remember saying to myself when she threw a left hand, 'That will do it—that will sway it now for her.'

It was that close. But maybe Katie was cautious in the final, but it was a big, big day. It's funny, but I was never nervous about Katie, and I would normally be nervous about those I know, hoping they will do well. I think they knew each other too well from previous meetings. Katie was just marvellous.

But I disliked the Russian opponent's attitude after the bout, claiming she was robbed and refusing to shake hands with Katie. Talk about being a spoilt brat throwing her toys out of the pram! I don't like people who say negative things after a match or after they lose . . . To Hell with them, unless they are robbed, and there are very few robberies now.

For example, as I briefly mentioned earlier, I don't think Kenny Egan was robbed. I think the Chinese man won it, and Kenny would have been a close friend of mine at the time, and I still tell him I don't think he won it, that he probably lost by a point or two. He would say, 'It's hard to argue with you.' But he's still convinced he was robbed.

Katie was just brilliant throughout London 2012 and I have no doubt that she will repeat history at the next Olympics. I went down to see her after one of the fights, I think it was the semi-final. She was walking up the corridor from the dressing-room and she came up to me. I just wanted to say, 'You're terrific,' to her, because although I am at the fights I never actually get to speak to the fighters. She came straight up to me and she asked, 'Was I okay?'

And I said to myself, 'That is modesty and humility.' I replied to her, 'You were better than okay, Katie. You were brilliant.'

'Thank you. That's wonderful. Thank you,' she said with great modesty.

I think it is very hard to repeat things in any walk of life, and even if you repeat success you are only repeating what you have already done, and the alternative is to go pro. I think if Katie maintains her present level or increases it she will be very hard to beat at the next Olympics. There will be others coming along in the next three years, between now and Rio de Janeiro. Katie is a good lesson for aspiring boxers. If you watch her she is on her feet all the time; she is the finished article. But only a fool would bet against Katie winning again in Rio in 2016.

I remember going up one evening to Belfield with my grandson to see Katie playing in a football match. During the game I said, 'See that girl there? She is going to win the world championship in a couple of weeks.' I think it was the Europeans that were coming up, and she duly won and hasn't lost since. Olympics, world, European and European Union, she has won them all.

After the Olympic final I asked her father, Pete, and Katie if she would launch the book, and she said Yes, even though she had other things on her mind. Book launches are always special occasions, but this one was all the more special because it was actually the first public appearance Katie made after winning gold at the Olympics. At the launch in September 2012 she said some very kind words about me to the press. 'I don't think you can mention Irish sport without mentioning Jimmy Magee. He's a legend in Irish sport, and for me personally he's been such a great support to me over the years, and to my family as well. Even when women's boxing was unheard of in the country he was always there supporting me right from the start.'

I seem to remember she arrived back in Ireland from holidays only the day before the launch. That was a wonderful night, and the setting in the Aviva Stadium was perfect. So I was delighted with that. To have my book launch as the first thing she did on her return was a nice thank you—not that she had anything to thank me for.

Chapter 20 ~

| AROUND THE WORLD

Without exaggerating, I'd say I've travelled more than a million miles and visited more than eighty-five countries in my broadcasting career, which is thankfully still going strong after six decades. In 1977 I even went on my own world tour to see up close many of the iconic stadia around the globe. When I think about the stand-out moments in sport I also always think of the electrifying atmosphere, which is usually the effect of the great cities and venues where these historic events took place. Great cities can be a *different class*, and wide-ranging.

———

New York is my favourite city on the planet. It is a fantastic place in every sense. It is a cosmopolitan melting-pot. You can get any food from anywhere in the world, from burgers (horseburgers, beefburgers, chickenburgers) to fine dining. If you have never been to New York I recommend you to go.

You arrive in either Newark Airport or JFK, and there is something special about it when you get into a taxi and head across town. There's a buzz about the place that you get as soon as you leave JFK Airport and head towards the bright lights of the big city on the Long Island expressway. Without fail, the excitement builds for me as I pass the famous Shea Stadium, where the New York Mets used to play, and go through the Queens Bridge; and then the magnificent skyline of Manhattan suddenly appears. Without fail it awakens special feelings in me. I don't know if that comes from the fact that I was born in New

York and spent the first three years of my life there before my parents got homesick and moved back to Ireland.

Virtually everywhere, every landmark would be known to you, either through films or television. So even if you never visited New York you would still be familiar with all the places, such as Central Park, Fifth Avenue, Madison Avenue, the Empire State Building, St Patrick's Cathedral, the Rockefeller Centre and of course Yankee Stadium—the same stadium that you used to hear about, with this fantastic pulling power. They have now built a new stadium and—a very American way of doing things—demolished the old stadium and right beside it built the new Yankee Stadium.

The 1947 All-Ireland final, between Kerry and Cavan—the only one to be played outside Ireland—was played at the Polo Grounds, which is now a housing estate. That particular game is a special one for me. I was eleven years old, listening to it on the wireless, and I'll always remember thinking during the game that I wanted to be a sports commentator when I grew up. I sometimes have to pinch myself when I think that not only did my dream come true but I actually got to cover many major sporting events in this fabulous city that helped kick-start my imagination about a career in broadcasting.

My favourite venue is probably Madison Square Garden, and I have worked there. Opened in 1968, it is now in its third or fourth incarnation. It might have begun life in Madison Square, but it is not there now; the venue that bears its name these days is over near Pennsylvania Station, between Seventh and Eighth Avenues. I was there the night Eamonn Coghlan got a standing ovation. I couldn't believe how much they loved him. Today it is home to the New York Knicks, and it hosts more than three hundred events each year.

In the older days the Garden had some of these great American fights; there was Jack Dempsey, Ali, Tyson, Robinson and Roy Jones. It has also hosted many memorable concerts by the likes of Elvis, Chuck Berry, the Rolling Stones, Bruce Springsteen, the Police, Pearl Jam and John Lennon; in fact it is the venue where the former Beatle last performed.

New York will be best remembered by Irish soccer fans for our famous victory over Italy at USA '94 in the Giants Stadium. Technically the stadium isn't in fact in New York but across the river in New Jersey.

———

Second on my list of cities that I would describe as a *different class* is Cape Town, South Africa. It is an absolutely stunning place. In fact I think I would like to live there. The city is backdropped by the picturesque Table Mountain. If you had to furnish your city the way people furnish homes they would be trying to buy mountains like Table Mountain to put into their city to make it look better to visitors. It is fabulous.

If you go down to the V&A (Victoria and Alfred) Waterfront you see a whole new reclaimed area, with magnificent shops and restaurants. It is a deep-sea port, and the cruise liners come right into the centre of the city. You can get a boat out during the day to Robben Island, where Nelson Mandela was incarcerated for twenty-seven years. The little tours they do are guided by former inmates, which makes its dark history really hit home.

It is a *different class* when it comes to hotels, particularly the Mount Nelson Hotel. Another fine hotel is the Table Bay Hotel, right down in the harbour, which is the city's beating heart. Speaking of hearts, Cape Town is home to the hospital where Christiaan Barnard performed the first heart transplant in 1967.

It's also home to a famous cricket and rugby grounds, the Newlands. The venue is steeped in history. I couldn't count the number of great teams that played here. Irish men have played here with the Lions; and Tony O'Reilly still holds the record for tries here.

Cape Town was one of the venues for the last football World Cup in 2010. Unfortunately Ireland didn't get to South Africa, because of the infamous double hand-ball episode by Thierry Henry during the play-off with France in Paris. The Irish team played France off the pitch that night, which made the episode all the more gut-wrenching. Anyway, I will remember the South African World Cup for the wonderful football, particularly by Spain, the deserved winners. It's rarely that the team that is most attractive to the eye wins these tournaments.

Chapter 21 ~

| DIFFERENT-CLASS CITIES

The third place on my list of *different-class* cities is Hong Kong, which is another one of those places fashioned by nature and money but essentially by nature. It is a real harbour. The old airport was right in the centre of the city, and you could almost read the labels on the clotheslines as your flight descended. The old Templehof in Berlin was the same.

Hong Kong is fascinating, to say the least. It is essentially two parts: Hong Kong Island and Kowloon. When you climb up Victoria on the shuttle railway and you have the overview back down to the city it is truly spectacular.

I've had the privilege of staying in hundreds of hotels during my career. It really has become a hobby of mine to visit hotels around the world that I would describe as not just top class but a *different class*. Hong Kong does not disappoint on this front either. There is the Mandarin on the Hong Kong side, and then you can get the Star Ferry across to the Peninsula Hotel, which is one of the very, very best in the world. One of the great things in Hong Kong is the Star Ferry. You can go to Macau, the former Portuguese island that is now back in Chinese hands, for the gambling if you want to gamble; and if you want to eat, what a place! This picturesque island off Hong Kong's coast is probably best known to film buffs for Bruce Lee's film *Game of Death* and the James Bond film *The Man with the Golden Gun*.

There are two big race-courses in Hong Kong that are out of this world. There's Sha Tin, which is out on the edge of the New Territories; the other one, Happy Valley, is right underneath the towering blocks in the city centre. A lot of Irish jockeys go there during the Irish off-season.

Golf courses there are unbelievable too. As the old adage goes, money talks, and it certainly talks here. And of course you can buy anything you like, from suits of clothes to bits and pieces.

——

The first European city on my list, at number 4, is Berlin, which is a mighty place. It always was a fantastic city, but then the Second World War came and made a mess of it, and then it was a divided city, but even then it was a fascinating place to visit. You could go through Checkpoint Charlie, which was amazing to do and go into the old East Berlin. There is a fabulous hotel there called the Adlon, which is now part of the Kempinski group. It was sort of lost to the 'bling' generation when Berlin was divided but now it is top of the range. It is right beside the Brandenburg Gate. You can look out the window while eating your breakfast and see the gate.

The stand-out sites for me include the Rotes Rathaus (Red City Hall), which was built in the late nineteenth century, inspired by the architecture of the Renaissance. I adore the new railway station, which they built on the site of part of the old Berlin Wall. Thankfully they have cleared all that area. There is no dereliction there. The station is the new Hauptbahnhof and is impressive with its steel-and-glass structure. I'm also fond of the old Kaiser Wilhelm Memorial Church in the Kurfürstendamm in the centre of the Breitscheidplatz. It is the famous church that was bombed in 1943 during the war, and they have left the damaged spire as it is and put in a memorial hall.

Of course Berlin hosted the Olympic Games in 1936, when Jesse Owens won his four gold medals, and the World Cup in 2006. There was no Irish team at the 1936 Olympics, because there was the usual row about something. On that occasion it had to do with the North and South; it was literally a case of 'What is Ireland?' These internal quarrels happened mostly in athletics, where it was a problem, because if you wanted to be from Northern Ireland you had to go with the NACA body, which was not recognised internationally. They only recognised the 26 Counties; so you can imagine what it was like in 1936. Imagine what it would be like now, even!

——

Fifth on my list of favourite cities is the spectacular Rio de Janeiro. I have visited it many times, and I hope to be back there, please God, in 2014 to cover the World Cup. Rio is something else; it is a *different class*. From the moment you get to the airport in Rio you can't be unaware of its place in the football world. You get a taxi, and the driver will switch on the radio to listen to the game and you'll hear the commentator going hysterical, completely overboard, screaming the famous 'Goooal' catchphrase that is part of the tradition in that part of the world.

I don't have this on good authority—it is more on my own authority (which is not very good). If you ever wondered what is the origin of that, I believe I have a possible reason for it. So dense is the traffic and so noisy are the people that if you were listening to a game on your house radio or car radio you would never know there was a goal scored without the commentator screaming in such an over-the-top fashion. I think it began so that anyone driving around would know there had been a goal at the Maracanã stadium.

On my first trip to Rio I received an unexpected welcome from Pelé. I'd gone to visit a broadcaster friend of my mine named Walter at TV Global, and he said to me, 'There's somebody I want you to meet. There is a very special man who wants to say hello to you, Jimmy.' And he pressed the button on the studio's control and Pelé popped up on the screen to say in a recorded video message: 'Jimmy, you are welcome to Brazil.' Years later Pelé would tell me that he remembered recording that lovely welcome message for me.

One of the best views is by the Christ the Redeemer statue, the famous statue with a fantastic view over the Pão de Açúcar (Sugarloaf Mountain) and of the sea there. However, the best view of all is from the favelas (shanty towns) on the hillside. If you can get up there, there is a fantastic view.

When you get into Rio itself there is a continuous chain of beaches that follow one another; there is Botafogo, Ipanema, Copacabana . . . it is just a stunning place, and everybody is playing either volleyball or football on the beach. They play from when the sun comes up until it goes down. There must be some law and order attached to it, because the same people can't be playing all the time!

I was told one time there was a famous man and if you were lucky you might see him playing on the beach. As it turns out I was lucky and I saw this man playing, the famous man with the bent legs, Manuel Francisco dos Santos, known as Garrincha (which means Little Bird). He had deformed legs and had one of these rheumatic things when he was young. I'm not sure what it was, but he was born with it, and it left him with deformed legs, where they both moved in the same direction. It would be impossible to be an athlete, you would think, yet he turned out to be one of the best footballers Brazil ever had. He played in the World Cup in 1958 when they won it for the first time, in Sweden. He was in it again four years later in Santiago in Chile. The fans named him the Angel with Bent Legs. He had a few other nicknames, including Joy of the People and Mané Garrincha. They even named the home team's dressing-room after him in the famous Estádio do Maracanã.

I got to see him playing on the beach; he was there with a load of youngfellas, playing away. He was slightly eccentric, to say the least; for it's hard to imagine a top-class professional footballer playing football on the beach with a group of youngsters. Even back then I'd imagine any manager would drop dead from a heart attack if they saw one of their star players having a kick-around on the beach.

It was said that he was very fond of the female form, and extremely fond of the drink form, and sadly he was dead by the time he was fifty. I didn't talk to him, but it was fascinating to see him playing there.

The Irish team played in Brazil back in 1982 under my friend Eoin Hand. Brazil had a top-notch team, and Ireland—it goes without saying—hadn't. But we didn't even have a decent squad on that tour of South America, because Eoin found it virtually impossible to get his good players to go, because they were in their closed season and they wanted time off with their families. It was a big defeat, 7-0! Brazil were Brazil. I wasn't at that game, because it was a time when nobody really went to far-flung exotic places with the Irish team; there was no press corps as such. We also lost 1-0 to Chile and 2-1 to a very bad Trinidad and Tobago side during that disastrous tour.

We eventually became the first Celtic country to beat Brazil, in Lansdowne Road back in 1987, with a great goal from Liam Brady. I can't emphasise enough how beautiful that goal was. It was spectacular.

I can't wait for the next World Cup in Brazil. Sadly, it doesn't look as if Ireland will be playing there, because it's highly unlikely that we'll pull off the miracle of getting out of our qualifying group.

Speaking of highly embarrassing defeats, perhaps the biggest the Irish team ever endured in recent times was in the World Cup qualifying game in October 2012 against Germany in Lansdowne Road. This 6-1 defeat was our biggest loss ever on home soil.

Swiftly moving the subject away from that nightmare and back to Brazil, I have to say that this fabulous city has some beautiful hotels. The one that stands out for me is the Copacabana Palace, where all the A-listers used to go, and still go. It is Hollywood hierarchy; think of any star, and they went there. This luxury hotel is on the famous Copacabana beach.

I remember on my first trip to Rio I was warned to be very careful of any guys polishing shoes. I've seen them, and they were smooth operators. You'd have a group of four or five children running around, and one of them asks you if you want your shoes polished. You automatically say No, but it doesn't deter him from putting a big dollop of polish on your shoe, and you are left with this ugly mess on your best summer shoes. The next guy comes over and apologises and spreads the polish, and then before you know what the hell is going on another guy comes and starts polishing your shoes. By the time this is all played out you'll have reached the end of the street. Quite frankly, most tourists were afraid of them and would quickly hand them over some loose change and would let out a sigh of relief when the gang would go away and leave you alone. It was the first time I came across this, and I found it an interesting concept.

Rio has one of the best stadia, in the shape of the famous Maracanã, which staged the World Cup final in 1950. The World Cup story began in 1930 in Uruguay; in 1934 it was held in Italy and in 1938 it was held in France; and then the war broke out, so the next time it was held was in 1950, in Brazil, and the final was played in the Maracanã stadium, with nearly 200,000 people attending. Some sources say there were more than 200,000, but they have re-examined the records and have now settled on a figure of 198,000. It is still the biggest crowd ever to watch a football match. This is where the final will be held in 2014.

I have seen some great matches there. It's like going to Mecca: it is a fantastic arena. I saw Flamingo and Botafogo playing there, as well as a few international matches. I saw Brazil with such players as Careca and Jairzinho playing Ecuador in 1976 on my world tour. The stadium was only half full, but the atmosphere was still amazing.

I think they might have better health and safety there now. It was built specifically for the World Cup in 1950, but it wasn't quite finished, and they got thousands of people to work on it in the last few weeks, hoping it wouldn't fall down! It was really pressed with that sort of crowd. As it happened, Brazil had a wonderful World Cup in 1950, but they didn't win it; that honour went to Uruguay, thus Brazil has never won it on their home soil.

2014 will be the second time for Brazil to host the World Cup. They were hot favourites in 1950 but probably won't be next year. My favourites to win at this moment are Spain, Germany or Argentina. The South American side are sensational at the moment, including Messi. Only eight countries have ever won the World Cup: Uruguay, Italy, Germany, Brazil, England, Argentina, France and Spain. It's a very select group.

Withdrawn From Stock
Dublin Public Libraries

Chapter 22 ∿

|WHAT A TRIP!

Argentina is another very special country. You see the places and connections with Ireland as you go through the towns. I was told they speak English with an Irish accent still in some parts of the country.

9th of July Avenue is the big wide avenue right through the centre of Buenos Aires. It is said to be the widest street in the world; but I haven't been to every street in the world, so I don't know, and we'll have to take it at face value. The famous Colón Theatre is there also. If you are going to Buenos Aires you must go to La Boca, where they do the tango. It is said to be the birthplace of the tango, and even those who only do it in an amateur way would be thrilled to show you how to do it. Buenos Aires is just a brilliant place, and with great restaurants.

I did the Field Hockey World Cup there in 1978. I had been there the previous year, and I was also there for the football World Cup in 1978, where I saw some great matches. I was interviewed on television once at La Bombonera (which means the chocolate box), which is the home ground of Boca Juniors. There was a match in the Copa Libertadores— the South American cup—between Boca Juniors and another South American club. An Argentine friend of mine asked if I could do a few words with him on live television down on the pitch. He talked to me about looking forward to the game and about who might win. I told him, 'I think Boca will win by 3-0.' My predication was correct. Of course, I was blessed.

Five days later I was back in the same city again, where Argentina were playing an international. It just shows you how lucky you can be with a prediction, because by this time everyone was talking about this analyst from Ireland who said that Boca would win 3-0, and so I was asked again for television who I thought would win in that night's game. I said I thought they would come away with at least a three-goal victory and maybe 4-1. And sure didn't Argentina win the game 4-1!

I have many fond memories of Buenos Aires, where I first witnessed Diego Maradona playing when he was sixteen years old in a game in which Argentina Juniors were playing Velez Sarsfields. At half time a sub came on. He was a little tubby for a young guy, with bushy kind of hair. But he was just sensational. I said to myself, 'This fella is unbelievable; he can do anything.' I knew that he was going to be an international sensation. I was eventually proved right when Maradona arrived on the international scene in 1982 and single-handedly beat England in 1986 with his *different class,* as I described him when doing the commentary on that game. The only player from Argentina who has come near him since has been Lionel Messi.

———

In seventh place of my list of all-time favourite cities is Barcelona. I have great memories of the Olympic Games there in 1992. It was just a magnificent view on Montjuïc, which overlooks the city, and you can go up to it by cable car, down from the port. I have been there a good few times. I went there to see the athletics championships and the world swimming championships—and not in my capacity as a commentator but rather as an ordinary fan, paying for these trips out of my own pocket.

I have also done football matches there at the Camp Nou ('New Field'). I saw Barcelona in action at a time when Cruyff was in charge. They always had great teams. I remember when Bobby Robson was manager and was very good to me, extraordinarily helpful, which I will never forget him for. I was able to thank him for that when he came over here as part of the management team with Steve Staunton.

Pep Guardiola is no doubt one of the best managers they had. He was a wonderful player for them also, and he knew them inside out, because he knew the club; he *was* the club. He came as a boy, stayed on as a player, and left at the right time when they were completely on top. Unfortunately, the man who took over was forced to resign in August 2013 due to his battle with cancer. As a side note, an Irishman named Patrick O'Connell, who was the first Irish player to captain Manchester United, actually managed Barcelona back in the mid-1930s, when the Spanish Civil War was going on. He won titles with them too and took them on a famous trip to Mexico and the United States as a fund-raising effort to keep the club afloat.

———

Perhaps surprisingly, I place Vienna ahead of many of the obvious favourite European cities, such as Paris and London. If you think of Vienna maybe you think of the Harry Lime theme; maybe you think of *The Third Man* and the zither, an instrument with a guitar-like sound. The big Ferris wheel is also symbolic of Vienna. But there is also some great football played there—football for the purist. The Austrian team used to be one of the greatest teams, and Vienna was its home. It is also the home of the great Vienna State Opera House and also the Schönbrunn Palace, the hotel that originated the *torte* (chocolate cake), and the Vienna Boys' Choir. There are so many things to think of in Vienna!

———

Paris is ninth on my list. When you are talking about cities of this calibre, Paris is a must. It stands out for so much: there's the culinary side, the fashion side, the famous landmarks and the sports side. Every time I think of Paris I can see the organ-grinder at the top of Montmartre, just outside the walls of Sacré-Cœur, playing Édith Piaf's 'La vie en rose'.

On the sports front the biggest occasion has to be the city's hosting of the finish of the Tour de France every year. I was lucky enough to see Stephen Roche win it in 1987. Some people jokingly claim Charlie

Haughey won it, as he was at the finishing line so quickly! He was there to present Roche with a hug at the end. Imagine winning the Tour de France! Paris has lots of memories for me, but without a doubt the biggest is seeing Stephen Roche at the finishing line.

We've had some major wins in rugby there too. The stand-out moment was in 1999 when O'Driscoll scored three tries. Every time you do that in Paris it is a big one, and that is definitely a *different class*. Brian is one of the greatest players who ever played for Ireland, or, for that matter, in the world. But that day he adorned the whole occasion by getting over with three tries. I mean, how many people in Six Nations have gone over to Paris and scored three tries? You can certainly count them on the fingers of your two hands, that's certain.

Paris is also a place where Ireland has played some very good football. During the Giles era we were robbed on one occasion with an offside goal that wasn't offside. If we had won that particular game we would have topped the group, with a couple of games to go, and perhaps made it to a World Cup before the Charlton era. It seemed like a case of history repeating itself when Trapattoni's team were knocked out of World Cup qualification. It's also a crying shame that Ireland never qualified for the 1998 World Cup, staged in Paris. It would have been a fantastic occasion for our fans.

Paris is also, of course, where Eoin Hand had great success with the Irish team. It was where he discovered Michael Robinson, who managed to get an Irish passport shortly before the game. Robinson played for Liverpool and went to Spain at the end of his career and became a very popular football pundit.

Coming home from the first Paris trip, Hand said to him, 'If you really want to be a true Irishman you have to learn some of these old Irish songs.' He sent him over to me so I could teach him. As a joke, I began singing in sean-nós style to him, which was basically me mumbling and every now and then singing the words 'factory wall'. He listened attentively and later reported back to Hand: 'I can't understand anything. All I can hear is mumbling and then saying the bloody "factory wall" over and over again!' Unfortunately for Robinson, Eoin told him that's what he would have to sing, and to learn it syllable by syllable and word for word.

———

London has to be in my top ten, though just scraping in. I have a lot of very fond memories of the English capital. I suppose the most recent would be the fabulous occasion in the ExCel Arena when Katie Taylor became the first Irishwoman to win a boxing gold medal. The London Olympics in general were just wonderful for me and never to be forgotten.

London was also where I was sent on my first foreign assignment to do a commentary on the FA Cup. It just happened to be the all-London Cup final of 1967 between Tottenham Hotspur and Chelsea. It was actually the first FA Cup final between two London teams.

It was also at the London Olympics that I was presented with a special award for having attended the greatest number of Olympic Summer Games. There were awards for those who had attended ten or more Games, and there were a few of us. I'm now at eleven Olympics. Funnily enough, not a lot of people have attended eleven Olympic Games, and most of those being presented with their awards were print journalists, with not many broadcasters.

I could go on and on about London. It's been a very special city for many Irish footballers who have made the grade there down through the years. Who am I thinking of? The names that immediately spring to mind are Paddy Mulligan, Frank Stapleton, David O'Leary, Liam Brady, Terry Neill, Pat Jennings . . . The list goes on.

It's a city that's almost synonymous with boxing. It was here that Barry McGuigan fought for the world featherweight title against Eusébio Pedroza of Panama back in 1985. The Panamanian boxer at that point had had a long career, having lost only one fight before meeting the Irishman. He had defended his world title a couple of dozen times before he was abruptly stripped of it by McGuigan. I will certainly never forget it anyway. Doing the commentary on that match was special, because I knew the McGuigan family for years and had keenly followed Barry's career from the start.

He was brilliant. When McGuigan had you going you stayed going—that was certain. When he hurt you, you stayed hurt. He was a fabulous puncher, and he could also take it. He essentially started from nothing, apart from talent, which is the most priceless commodity of them all.

People talk about training facilities, but McGuigan—just like Katie Taylor—didn't have wonderful training facilities. He was training out in the back of a shop in Clones, but he worked at it and he made it his. He is one of those who are lucky enough to be in the International Boxing Hall of Fame in Canastota, in New York State. We have nobody else of equal value there: there may be one or two of the oldie guys from way, way back, like Jack Dempsey, but none of the modern players are in there at all.

———

Chicago—'that toddlin' town', as it's called in an old song by Fred Fisher—conjures up many sporting moments, which is why I have it as my eleventh favourite city in the world.

The famous 'Long Count' between Jack Dempsey and Gene Tunney took place in Chicago. It was a world heavyweight title fight, and a new rule had come in. At one time when you had a knock-down you could stand over your opponent and wait for him to move or to get up and then clatter him again, but this new rule meant that you had to go to a neutral corner on a knock-down, the same as it is now. Dempsey put Tunney down and didn't retreat, but the referee wasn't familiar with the rule, and by the time he got Dempsey to return to his corner it was reckoned by ringside observers that the count would have been 14 had it begun when it should have, because Tunney was then up before the official count of 10. So it got a nickname—as is typical of America—'the Long Count'. Tunney got up and duly won the fight.

Twice they fought for the world title and twice Tunney 'won'—both times on points, and each time over ten rounds, but really Dempsey knocked him out in their first bout except for the Long Count.

When in Chicago you can go to the Soldier Field stadium to watch the Chicago Bears. You can catch a basketball game with the Chicago Bulls at the United Center and see the court on which the great Michael Jordan played. He is probably the best basketball player who ever lived, and has the medals to prove it from the NBA, but more importantly he has two Olympic gold medals as the heart of the Dream Team in 1992 in Barcelona.

It's not all about sports in Chicago. The Magnificent Mile is a great shopping place. There are the little nightclubs that were owned by, or allegedly owned by, Al Capone. There is one called the Green Mill, which is just outside the city; a $22 taxi journey (I don't know how I still know that), and the holes are still in the wall from shotgun fire when the Feds came looking for Al. It is now a very good jazz club. I really love Chicago; it's a great place to be, and it gives New York a run for its money.

———

Another American city that would make my list of top fifteen is San Francisco. The things I like most about this city are the cable cars, Fisherman's Wharf, Nob Hill, Alcatraz and the beautiful Golden Gate Bridge. I have done football matches there in the USA '94 World Cup, which was wonderful.

———

Number thirteen on my list is Budapest, Hungary. I remember being at the world and European Champions boxing championships in Budapest—not at the same time, I must stress! On the first occasion a fella called Casey won a medal for Ireland in the Europeans, and in the world championship a lad called Stephen Kirk won a light-heavyweight medal for Ireland. On that second occasion in Budapest they announced that they had a couple of celebrities in the house, and the

MC mentioned two people in particular: one was a guy called László Papp, their greatest boxer ever, and the place went mad—and rightly so, because he was the first man to win three gold medals at Olympic boxing (at London in 1948, Helsinki in 1952 and Melbourne in 1956). He got a rousing reception, but it was topped by the reception for the next man. 'Give a nice welcome, please, for Ferenc Puskás, former captain of the Hungarian team.' He wouldn't be a regular in that stadium, but God did he get some reception! It was just mighty. He left his home town after the Soviet invasion in 1956, when a lot of them scarpered, and he finally came back. You could see that they loved him. They have now named the main stadium after him; it was called Népstadion (People's Stadium) and is now called Ferenc Puskás Stadium. He scored an amazing eighty-four goals in eighty-five inter-national games, won an Olympic medal, played for Real Madrid, scored more than half a dozen goals in the European Championship Cup final, and even scored a goal in a World Cup final. If we had a player that good we'd probably have named half of Dublin after him!

———

The third-last city on my list is Stockholm. It's another lovely city with an Olympic Games connection: the 1912 Games were held there. There was a hotel built especially to house visitors for those Games, and I was told that if you go to a certain room in the hotel you can see across the waters (Stockholm is built on water) to the apartment where Ingrid Bergman lived. Now, I am a big fan of Bergman. Sure what man wouldn't be? So I went to the hotel and asked them if it was true, and I went to the room and looked across. Now, whether it was her place or not I don't know, but to satisfy myself I said it was.

———

Moscow is second-last on my list. I said earlier that great cities can be architectural masterpieces, and I think Moscow more than meets this criterion. Obviously it has the distinction of being politically a very important place in world history, but it was also the site of the Olympic Games in 1980, when poor oul' Eamonn Coghlan was very unlucky to lose out on a medal for a second time. John Treacy had a good run in the 10,000 metres in 1980. Leaving the Olympic Games, there have been a few football matches there that I attended that were very enjoyable.

———

Last, but by no means least, is Sydney. The stand-outs for me are Darling Harbour, Sydney Harbour Bridge, the famous Opera House, the Rocks, and the Manly Ferry. The Olympic Games in 2000 were among the most beautiful Games. Every morning to go to work I had to cross the Harbour Bridge in a double-decker train. It was wonderful, a breathtaking sight to behold. They named all the little streets around the Olympic sites after famous Australians: Herb Elliott Avenue, Dawn Fraser Avenue, and various athletes who were also a *different class.*

———

I'm in my sixth decade as a broadcaster, which according to those in the know makes me the longest-serving sports commentator in the English-speaking world. As I mentioned earlier, I've travelled more than a million miles and visited eighty-five countries, but I still get a buzz any time I jump on a plane and enter a stadium to cover any sports event. Reflecting back on my broadcasting career, I still have to pinch myself to realise how privileged I was to be present at so many of the great sporting moments that I have outlined here as being worthy of putting into the *different class* category.

Leabharlanna Poibli Chathair Bhaile Átha Cliath
Dublin City Public Libraries

INDEX